Every Inch Love Will

by Meredith Coleman McGee

Copyright © 01.02.2022 Meredith Coleman McGee
Foreword by Starry Krueger
Introduction by Starkishia
Cover design (blue) Loretta Ealy

Meredith *Etc*
1052 Maria Court
Jackson, MS 39204-5151
www.meredithetc.com

First printing - Hardback & Softcover editions
Interiors–1 full color and 2 black & white
ISBN-13: 978-1-7341578-4-0 Kindle Direct Publishing
ISBN-13: 978-1-7378843-1-6 Printed by Ingram Spark
ISBN-13: 978-1-7341578-3-3 Barnes & Noble Press
88 images and photos
230 pages – 47, 073 words
a Memoir

Available on the World Wide Web as an eBook
All rights reserved. Submit written or electronic documents requesting use of any section of this work to the publisher.

Keywords: Black male, memoir, marriage, love affair, Mississippi writer, grief, JOBS Syndrome

Made and bound in the USA

Every Inch Love Will

by Meredith Coleman McGee

Meredith Etc
a small press

Blog: meredithetc.com
facebook Meredith Etc
🐦 Meredith*etc*

[Every Inch Love Will – Meredith Etc](#)

Make comments on the book page!

DEDICATION

Dedicated to the memory of William Earl McGee Jr.
August 28, 1965 – June 2, 2021
Jackson, Mississippi
Age 55

CONTENTS

PAGES

	DEDICATION	iv
	ACKNOWLEDGMENTS	vii
	FOREWORD	viii
	INTRODUCTION	xi
1	*The Stranger's Spring*	1
2	*Every Inch*	40
3	*Pandemic*	100
4	*May 30*	145
5	*Graveside*	160
6	*The Widow*	173
	Will's Family History Chart	213
	ABOUT THE AUTHOR	216

ACKNOWLEDGMENTS

First, I thank Jehovah for allowing me to spend 23 years and four months of my adult life with the one man who loved every inch of my existence. He loved my independent spirit, my neediness, my dreaminess, and my attentiveness to him. I loved his mind, body and soul and still do. He and I were faithful and loyal to our union.

I thank Loretta Ealy for the blue cover design; William Trest Jr. and Alice Paris for proofreading; and Starry Krueger for writing the Foreword and Starkishia for penning the Introduction. I thank the 15 widows one male Aaron Hodge, and 14 females who understood the gravity of my loss. I appreciate every visit, every call, every hug, and every smile. Rest in Heaven Hodge. He was laid to rest November 10, 2021, eight months after his loving wife. I thank the grief counselors including the VA Chaplain, my college friend Ella Lewis, mama, my aunts, uncles, friends, nieces, cousins, in-laws, and relatives who comforted me during this journey.

I was traumatized when Will died. My grief like a war wound has not healed yet. When Will closed his eyes, I entered a new chapter of my life as a widow. I gained new friends, old ones emerged, and others dropped completely out of sight.

In the words of my late husband: *I am moving one step ahead.* I am. As I put one foot in front of the other, I cherish my dear hearts unfulfilled dreams. He said: *Nobody can't stop me.* And on that note, *Nothing - not even death - stopped us.*

Happy reading!
Meredith Coleman McGee

FOREWORD

Every Inch Love Will is a love story, a story of a deeply devoted couple. Absorbing and moving, the story unfolds tenderly, in a local neighborhood as the two get to know each other and their families are knit together.

They don't take each other for granted. They are modest and appreciative about their good fortune in finding each other, having had broken relationships in the past. They commemorate their milestones and anniversaries and enjoy daily life. Although Meredith is often on the road for work, the story is about finding and keeping a home. As the author says about her husband, "Life placed me in his heart, next to his grandmother."

The book is also an account of their separate parallel lives as they change over time. One life shows the evolution of a woman at work -- her disillusionment with the nonprofit field and her emergence (in this order) as a typist, editor, author, publisher and entrepreneur extraordinaire. In tandem, her husband moves through several levels of a journeyman's life; he is a plumber and gains skills and credentials over time. The two maintained zones of privacy, not necessarily knowing details of the other's finances or income.

Underneath the happy story, there are low notes, reports of Will's medical afflictions, recurring like a beating drum, threatening the terrible loss to come. At one point, when the reader has been lulled into complacency by the fact that Will repeatedly recovers, it is shocking to learn that he has trouble holding a spoon.

I have had the honor and privilege of being acquainted with

the couple in this story. I know the author, who entered our rural leadership and education program when she worked at the Mississippi Association of Cooperatives, assisting Mississippi farmers.

The Rural Development Leadership Network (RDLN) is a national, multicultural social justice organization that supports community development in poor rural areas through hands-on projects, education, leadership development and networking. Participants take part in a four-week Rural Development Institute at the University of California, Davis; spearhead a project in their home areas during approximately two-and-a half years of involvement and have the option of earning an academic degree. (At the time of Meredith's participation, the master's was provided through Antioch University; it's now through the Great Plains Program, with the host being the University of Kansas.) Our Assemblies, held in diverse rural areas, provide the impetus for much of the travel described in this narrative.

Both Meredith and Will participated in activities of the Rural Development Leadership Network, and I witnessed their interaction, when, for example, Will would help with the transport and arrangement of Meredith's books for sale at events, or when I stayed overnight at their house and saw her solicitation for him.

After Will died, Meredith made the project of writing a memoir of their life together a way to work through her grief. She seems to have attacked the project with practicality and a natural determination, simply taking one step after the other, as she has taken on other projects in her life, like training citizens in redistricting while on the staff of Southern Echo, or like starting a family investment club, or undertaking initiatives to encourage literacy among children in Jackson, Mississippi, or joining book fairs there to make reading a priority for everyone (and to help sell books), or like assuming primary responsibility for the care of her infirm father under her roof. Caring for a parent is a big responsibility and she barely alludes to it in the book, taking it in stride.

A kind of confidence is needed for her approach, a willingness to learn by doing, not to know all the answers before starting out. Many of us are intimidated by academia, for example, held back by self-doubt or past difficulties. Meredith took on the independent study in the RDLN/Antioch master's program without batting an eye. Maybe some of her confidence comes from having a famous uncle -- James Meredith -- who integrated the University of Mississippi in 1962, Maybe some of it comes from having three close relatives (her father, mother, and uncle) who are published authors.

Facing the project of moving on through life as a widow, Meredith again is practical. Will was talented with mechanical processes. Meredith's future starts with learning how to get the car fixed.

Starry Krueger, *President*
Rural Development Leadership Network
New York, NY
December 22, 2021

INTRODUCTION

When asked to write the introduction for such a special book, I was not only taken aback, but honored to be considered for such a big contribution to an amazing story. I met Mr. and Mrs. McGee in 2012 while searching for a publisher for my memoir. I was given a flyer for Meredith Etc by a coworker who stated that a young man was posting them in a local library. Turns out the young man was William Earl McGee Jr. Upon our initial meeting, I knew the McGees were a loving and inspirational couple. Mr. McGee would also become the first patient I cared for during my introduction into the medical field.

Every Inch Love Will is a miraculous memoir dedicated to and written for a magnificent man. This book tells a story of true love and devotion which spanned over 23 years. Will and Meredith shared an unbreakable bond that tested time. Throughout their marriage, they faced many trials. However, they held onto each other and challenged the world as one. They supported each other's endeavors and advocated for one another. He was her biggest fan and she, his. And what would you expect from a couple so deeply in love?

Will was a hardworking, well educated, and honest man. He provided for his family and was a wonderful role model to his son, nieces, nephews, and peers. Utilizing his trade in plumbing, Will employed many young men. He gave them an opportunity to earn an honest days' wage while also teaching them everything he knew in hopes that they too could become successful in the field. Will was a pillar of his community. Everyone who knew or encountered him instantly loved and trusted him. He was a big brother to many.

As a young child Will was sickly. However, his medical condition did not stop him from pursuing his interests. In adulthood, a crippling diagnosis often threatened his very existence. Though hospitalized on numerous occasions, Will stayed positive and on his feet with the help of his caregiving spouse. Following each hospital stay, he was blessed to return home to his family, regain his strength, and push forward. Nothing detoured him. It is said that God gives His toughest battles to His strongest soldiers. And that is exactly what Will was, a soldier. He fought long and hard until the day God called him to rest.

Will and Meredith were blessed to share many memories and special moments over the 23 years they spent together. What started as an encounter with a stranger blossomed into a love that many people don't get the opportunity to experience. Through tears and pain, joy and sorrow, sickness and health, their commitment to each other grew with every moment. Nothing can alter the connection they had. The raw emotion with which their story was written makes evident the fact that their souls are fused, and they will forever be one. Their story is the epitome of black love, and their love affair will last until the end of time.

Starkishia, RN, Author, Co-author
Starkishia: Estrella
Mary's Story & Song

Praise for Every *Inch, Love Will*

Black Love is often hidden in plain sight because it begins in places we frequent in our everyday lives, and it happens when Black men and women have truly made up their minds they want to love and be loved -- and that they are worthy of a mature, honorable, lifelong kind of love. This is the love described within the pages of *Every Inch Love Will* as Meredith McGee demonstrates -through her unique storytelling- how Black love is the everyday actions of everyday people in our everyday Black spaces, and it goes from the local to the eternal spaces within the heart.

Jolivette Anderson aka The Poet Warrior, Host & Founding Production Partner of Mississippi Vibes Open Mic Poetry Set, Jackson, Mississippi 1998 – 2003

A beautiful love story, a testament to how growth can come from grief, and a personal history are weaved into a narrative in this candid work, which also highlights much of Black American history. This book is so seamless, you'll feel like you're sitting down at the kitchen table and listening to McGee tell her story over a good meal, the room filled with both laughter and tears.

Emily Michie Birch, M.L.S. Librarian and former editor at Praeger Publishers

Every Inch Love Will is a heart touching love story. This fast-paced read is a memorial to the love between Will McGee and Meredith McGee. It warmed my spirit to learn how much they cherished each other. I can only imagine how difficult it was for Meredith to create this love story so soon after Will's death. The things we do for love...

Alice Paris, *Retired*
Tuskegee University/Federation of Southern Cooperatives

A compelling and riveting memoir of a love affair where both partners learn to respect and trust each other regardless of financial and health obstacles.

William Trest Jr., Author of two novellas
The New Populist Party and *Reverse Guilty Plea*

CHAPTER 1

The Stranger's Spring

The Stranger's Spring

>Where were you last night,
>When the rain pounded against my window and the loneliness sunk in?
>Did you know I was here?
>With no one to love me, no one to hold me,
>No one to talk to, 'cause you were gone and I alone?
>Where are you now?
>While the sun shines so pretty and the flowers bloom
>And I feel like Spring inside – so warm – so needed.
>I hear a knock on the door – this isn't you – what must I do?
>The stranger enters and he sits, and he sits,
>and I become comfortable.
>The stranger sits and he sits, and he holds me.
>The stranger sits and he sits, and he loves me, and I love him back.
>I feel like Spring inside – so warm – so fulfilled.
>The stranger is good.
>Goodbye my love, the stranger is here.

Meredith S. Coleman
March 18, 1998

I wrote the poem *The Stranger's Spring* 10 days after my first date, March 8, 1998, with Will. He became my sweet sticky thang.' I became his. He was roughly 5'8. I was 5'3 and a half. He weighed 165 pounds. I weighed 138 pounds. He is dark. I am brown skinned. He is muscular and athletic. I am muscular and nonathletic. He had been divorced for three years. I had never been married.

We laid eyes on one another for the first time in 1992 at T.S. & M Super Stop on California Ave. in the Shady Oaks Community close to Grove Park near the first Black Golf Course in the City of Jackson, Mississippi established in 1959 so Black golfers would not need to integrate the other golf courses. Will's Uncle Junior used to walk three blocks home after winning 6-foot golf prize trophies. He was athletic – great at golfing and boxing; he played in the Negro Baseball League in Brooklyn where he posed for a photographer in his official baseball gear. He returned unmaimed - familiar with northern white hostility.

I read *The Stranger's Spring* publicly at a poetry set called Southern Vibes Open Mic night at Hi-Lites owned by Chris Burkett which was across the street from Tougaloo College. C. Leigh McInnis and Jolivette Anderson-Douoning were MCs and the biggest poets in the house. David Brian Williams, Derrick Johnson, Jolivette, and C. Leigh organized those poetry programs. Poetry was a popular mode of expression in the 1990s. Today, McInnis is an Instructor of English at Jackson State University. Anderson-Douoning is a former educator, a poet, and renown spoken word artist. Derrick Johnson is the 19th President of the NAACP. I do not know what Williams is up to these days.

Back then, my esteemed community leaders were hosting intellectual activities in my hometown, and they were my influencers. Today, I'm the Chair of Community Library Mississippi. I organize poetry contests, coordinate speaking programs, and host monthly book club meetings for all ages. I started writing poetry in high school encouraged by my young English teacher at Hinds Agricultural High School. I even wrote a play back then.

One person sparks action in another. That's how it goes. Inspiration comes from many places; influence can even come from the mouth of babies. Will inspired me to complete my first novel and his memoir which brings my published work count to 10. He is in heaven telling another angel that his wife is the author of 10 books and the best one is about him.

When I was reintroduced to Will I was working at the Mississippi Association of Cooperatives (MAC) on Hamilton Street. Derrick Johnson was involved in the NAACP, and he was associated with Southern Echo. At some point, Southern Echo rented office space through our parent organization, the Federation of Southern Cooperatives to Southern Echo. Hollis Watkins, a former SNCC organizer was originally my co-worker at MAC.

Mr. Hollis conducted the first lunch counter sit-in in the State of Mississippi in 1960 at the direction of Bob Moses whom we lost July 26, 2021. Moses was the architect of Freedom Summer in 1964 which drew workers to Mississippi by the droves from across the country to register black voters. Mr. Hollis was organizing a new organization - Southern Echo - with Mike Sayers and Leroy Johnson while he was organizing farm cooperatives for MAC.

In the early days, Will was a bull. He was vibrant, athletic, and active. Will enjoyed learning what made me tick. I liked reading and poetry and music. We were learning things about each other. It was exciting. There was no time to look back at what he had done and who he had done it with or what I had done and who I had done it with. We were in 5th gear – full speed ahead!

On the evening in February of 1998, when I read my new poem, I was sitting beside Will in the Poetry Club. I told him I was going to the mic next. Then, I walked to the Open Mic and read *The Stranger's Spring*. I was pleasantly surprised by the reaction of women in the audience who clapped vigorously; one yelled loudly, "I'm leaving that niggah." As I walked from the podium, I received compliments from women seated at tables in the aisle on my walk back to my table. Will appeared pleased. He pulled the chair out and I sat beside him. We listened to the next performances as we sipped our drinks.

Once we returned to my house on Dewitt Ave Will asked to see the poem. I handed him the sheet of paper which I had typed on my new desktop computer which I kept on my dining room table. He read the poem. I think he was trying to figure out the story. I told him he was the stranger in the poem, and there was nothing literal about the characters in the poem. He hadn't taken me from anyone. In the end, he was proud to claim the poem. I had phone numbers in my purse when I saw him in at the club on February 8th. I was not in a relationship. None of the brief relationships I had before I met him lasted longer than John stayed in the army. I was literally afraid of men in general.

Our childhood friend Ann had been killed by someone she met at a club. We were afraid of strangers. Belinda and I went out with Ann before she met the man who took her life. Afterward, we went to Police Headquarters on Pascagoula St. and talked to Detective Butler of JPD four or five times about Ann's case. Losing Ann was traumatic for us. We felt her butchered demise in the pits of our stomachs. We talked endlessly about the facts of her case and the details we learned after our visits to Detective Butler's office. We wanted justice for Ann. Her death was a great loss to us, and it changed our faith in dating. Our stance was "we came together, and we will leave together." Our number one rule was, "drinks can never be unattended." Secondly, "We got to check him out."

My best friend Belinda thought highly of Will; she judged him by his mannerism. He was pleasant and mild tempered wearing a light blue, denim shirt and jeans on February 8th. His clothes were pressed meticulously with deep creases in his jeans. He was wearing a necklace, but he did not have any rings. Will's natural charm, Belinda's influence, the weaknesses of the other suitors placed Will on first base by Valentine's Day. I had lived alone in my house on Dewitt Ave. for nine years. My previous boyfriends had their own homes, women, children, businesses, and hustles. I had been engaged twice – I was left hanging once – I called the other good catch off – my bad – too late. Life goes on!

So, this is my version of how Will and I got started. That Sunday night on February 8, 1998, I sat at the bar next to an older man. He immediately looked at me and I saw a sparkle in his eyes; maybe he admired my youthful face or how my outer loose-fitting shirt complimented my small waist and thick hips; anyway, he offered to buy my friends and me a round of drinks, but he kept a steady gaze on me. Sandra smiled. Then she and Belinda sat down. He asked us what we wanted. We told him what we wanted. He ordered our drinks and eventually, Sandra or Belinda danced with someone on fast songs. I watched the drinks and sat at the bar because the drinks kept coming.

Eventually, I excused myself and walked to the women's restroom. My eyes caught Will's eyes, or his eyes caught mine. He was playing pool with Milton. They spoke and I spoke. Eventually, the older gentleman drank too many drinks because he went to sleep at the bar.

As soon as Will noticed the older gentleman had fallen asleep, Will walked up to my bar stool and he asked, "Hey how you are doing?"

"I'm good," I replied.

"Ain't you Mary. Didn't you use to run the store on California?"

"Yes," I replied." I remembered his face, but I didn't know his name.

"You remember me?" he asked.

"I do remember you. But I don't remember your name," I added.

"I'm Will. I used to come to your store to buy cigarettes," he said. "I only stopped if I saw your white Maxima," he added.

"You want to dance?"

"I said OKAY." We danced to about three records in a row. The last song was a slow song. I felt his vibe when we were dancing slowly. When the song ended, Will walked me to my bar stool and he gave me his phone number and I gave him mine.

Will told me, "Call me."

I replied, "Okay."

Then, the older gentleman woke up. He appeared a little

beside himself. He looked around for a few seconds; then he told us he was getting ready to go. We thanked him for treating us to drinks; he left the building I guess to go home. A few days passed and Belinda called and asked me had I heard from Will. I told her I hadn't. She asked me did I call him. I told her, "No I hadn't called yet."

Anyway, Will called my house that Thursday. He asked me how I was doing and wanted to know why I hadn't called him. I lied and said, I misplaced his number. I was glad he called. I assumed he had loose ends because it took him a few days to call me. He asked me what I had been up to. I told him I had just finished reading a book about Huey P. Newton. He told me he had never heard of Huey Newton, but he was going to ask his dad about him. The next time I talked to Will he told me his dad said Huey Newton was a Black Panther.

I told Will the pocketbook "Huey Newton and the Black Panther Party" was a good read because I read it in one day. He listened as I gave him a summary. Mainly, I was disappointed in Huey Newton's demise. He was shot down on the streets of Oakland in 1989 during the Crack Cocaine epidemic by a black male. Huey Newton, this great man, who had called gang truces in the late 1960's and early 1970's, organized his community, helped start free breakfast programs for black youth, and influenced men to protect the community was shot down by a member of the Black Guerrilla Family.

Anyway, Will and I decided to get together for the weekend. We agreed to meet at a pool room on West Street. My ex-boy friend's mother "Ma' Mae," went with me. We hung out sometimes. Her son Larry, who I dated from 1993 to 1997, had moved to Los Angeles, but Ma' Mae and I were close. When we walked in, I spotted Will shooting pool and we walked over to his table. I introduced him to Ma Mae. I knew many of the guys playing pool. I played pool pretty well. I hung out often at different pool rooms around the city with my god-sister Treda and co-workers Edgar and Brenda.

Jo Mo, a friend of mine, played pool too. He told me once, "You going to run the young ones off. Ain't no man gonna' want a woman who beat em' playing pool." JoMo was the first person who ever called Ma Mae "Little Egypt" which was her stage name. Ma Mae used to dance in the 1970s for local bands which were managed by Al Gibbs. I don't know if Jo Mo was right or not about playing pool well because I was having a dry spell.

Somehow the subject came up about age. Will told me he was 31 years old. I lied and told him I was 29. I didn't want to be older than him. He played pool pretty, good. He handled the balls with skill; he was wearing out his opponent. A day or two later I went by 2504 Newport Street and met his 4-year-old son, Traa, father Big Will, his Uncle Butch, Snake, Maurice, and Anthony. I spoke to his son and told him my name. His son said, "I know who you are. You are Mary." His grandfather said, "Miss Mary." He was in old school. I also met JoJo, Anthony's son. He was five or six. He and Traa used to race to the couch to sit beside me when I came to visit. I was so tickled.

Will stopped by my house unannounced. I stopped by his house unannounced too. One day I stopped by and introduced Will to my teenage cousin Jessica. As always, everyone was friendly. I stopped by another time with my three-year-old niece Khadiya who was visiting my mother for the summer in Pensacola, and they drove over to see me. From the moment Khadiya saw Will she ran to him and called him "daddy." He hugged her. I was so embarrassed. I told her, "He's not your daddy."

She wasn't hearing none of that. Traa heard her and he barked, "He ain't your daddy!" She continued to cling to Will and me and Big Will smiled at each other because Traa opposed her clinging; she made up in her mind Traa was going to share Will with her that day. Will entertained his son and Khadiya. Big Will said, "Oh I got another grandbaby. Come here baby." Big Will gave Will a little help. Over the years, Will and I took Khadiya to all her ROTC balls except her 12th grade ball. They had an unbreakable bond.

I don't think Will was in a serious relationship when we met. Will told me he prayed regularly to God for me after dancing with me at the 900 Club on February 8, 1998, which turned into our Dating Anniversary for the next 23 years. In fact, I originally met Will in 1992 at T S & M Super Stop a convenience store business I owned and operated on California Ave in the old Mayes Grocery Store building in the Shady Oaks Community. He came in most evenings and purchased a pack of Kool short cigarettes. He told me he immediately felt a connection to me in 1992. I said, "I couldn't tell."

Will told me he thought I was attractive and a good woman. "I had a feel for you from the time I first saw you," he told me. I couldn't tell he had any interest in me personally because he spoke to people when he walked in and by the time, he made it to the cash register he smiled, spoke, ordered the usual, and was on his way. I did notice him. He was a clean-cut working man usually dressed business casual. Only three of four men who frequented the store like Randy or Jeff had jobs. Most guys, including his cousin Spanky dressed casually in various baseball caps, and different brand clothing, etc. Everyone who came in and out of the store was cool. I never had any problems.

Will and I showered each other with gifts and entertainment twice in February - February 8th and February 14th which became a part of our annual ritual. I had so many teddy bears by our 21st dating anniversary that I asked Will not to buy me anymore. He slowed down, but he bought more teddy bears anyway. As I write this story, this day, July 23, 2021, I have every teddy bear – 24. I went into our bedroom and counted them. One is in my home office.

Will and I moved fast after Valentine's Day in 1998. I was at his house. He was at my house. He spent the night at my house. I spent the night at his house. One day Traa asked me, "Miss Mary you gonna' spend the night with us tonight. I was alarmed. Children are watching. During weekdays, his mother picked him up and took him to daycare on State Street in Tougaloo. Several times, she called and told Will she couldn't take Traa to school; so, I drove him and was late for work.

My mother found out and she loaned Will a yellow 1979 dodge which was sitting in the yard. Soon, the transmission went out and Will had a friend from Newport Street put a transmission in the car and he kept driving it. My sister Willa used to drive it; she and her husband Calvin had a new black truck. March 11th, Traa turned five-years-old. He wanted me to come to his birthday party at his great Aunt Odessa's house. I didn't feel it was appropriate to attend his party. Will walked from Williamson Street at his aunt's house to visit me. He told me they were still at the party.

His aunt stayed about four blocks from me. I thought it was sweet he walked from the birthday party to see me.

The first Saturday in May, Will allowed Traa to ride to Gadsden, Alabama with me for our Family Reunion. My grandmother Beulah stayed at her niece Eve's house. Traa slept in the room with me and my grandmother on a cot. He was treated like another member of the family. He had so much fun with my cousins jumping on the trampoline he did not want to go home. My grandmother said, "Oh' that little boy adores you."

Traa asked me if I was attending his graduation from kindergarten. Will and his ex-wife were co-parenting, and all those events were off limits to me. I was a friend. Will was daddy. She was mama. I was "Miss Mary." My name is not Mary, but I have been called Mary since June 1988 when I opened Sunrise Foods #2 in the Virden Addition Community. My Uncle Claudel owned Sunrise Foods on Deer Park. He taught me how to keep books, do inventory, and the whole nine yards before I opened a candy store enterprise from my mother's living room after college in 1987.

When I moved my business which I renamed TS & M Super Stop to Mobile St. and then California Ave, the name 'Mary' followed me. 'T' stood for Terry, my god sister Terry Holmes, 'S' stood for Sidney, my boyfriend when I moved to Mobile Street, and 'M' stood for Meredith. I could count on one hand, the customers who called me "Meredith."

On May the 15th, I went to Davis, California for a month-long stay at UC Davis to study Rural Community Development in a joint program sponsored through the university's Community Development Department (UC

Davis) and the Rural Development Leadership Network (NYC). The Federation of Southern Cooperatives raised the funds for my travel and expenses. I rented an apartment off campus for one month. I was to return June 16, 1998. The month-long trip did not sit well with Will. He was like you will be gone "a whole month."

I replied, "Yes," I'll be back." I was so excited to have the opportunity to go which meant I could obtain credit hours toward a master's degree. My co-worker Charlie, who worked for the Federation in the Albany office was the first choice and when he couldn't go Shirley Sherrod, the Director of the Albany office asked me if I wanted to go in Charlie's place.

Mama took a picture to *The Mississippi Link* newspaper, and they ran a story about my month-long study opportunity at UC Davis. Mama gave Minnie Garrett a picture of me wearing a tan felt hat. I fussed about mama's picture selection. I said, "Mama you couldn't find a better picture than that?"

"I don't see nothing wrong with that picture. It looks just like you," mama declared.

Of course, I wanted to attend the program. I explained to Will that I travelled on my job and why studying in Davis, CA was a great opportunity. My co-worker Daisy who worked with me on Hamilton Street off Farish Street downtown Jackson had gone to China in 1995 four months after I started working for the Mississippi Association of Cooperatives. Traveling was broadening my horizons. I was present at Neal's Lodges in Concan, Texas when RDLN honored Alice Paris for obtaining a master's degree in Rural Community Development. I went to Del Rio, Mexico with the group for dinner at Ciudad Acuna. We had authentic Mexican food which makes Taco Bell a joke.

Starry Kruger, President, RDLN, paid the dinner tab for the entire group. We crossed the border in a large bus. We stopped at Walmart in Del Rio, Mexico. I didn't have much money, but I spotted a caller ID phone which was only $10 so I bought it. Caller ID phones were $200 at home. My sister, Eva, complained because I didn't buy two. I hate to admit it, I didn't have a lot of money on that trip. We stayed in Concan, Texas at a retreat center. For the first time in my life, I was in the room with a group of multicultural activists – white, black, Hispanic, Indian. Everyone was sitting in a circle sharing.

While I was in Davis, I wrote Will, and I mailed him letters and mailed him several postcards. I called from pay phones when I had the opportunity. We talked on the phone whenever I could catch him at home. But I missed him often. His dad told me several times, "He just went to the store. Call back." Will wrote me one letter. I kept Will updated. He was interested in everything going on.

There were three other rural fellows in our group. Martha Beatty from North Carolina; Nancy Warneke from Montana; and Mike Acosta from Texas. Martha and Nancy shared an apartment. I had an apartment by myself two buildings from them. Mike had an apartment by himself two buildings right of my building. Our academic agenda was full. Martha rode the city bus to campus. Mike, Nancy, and I walked together to campus every day.

Once we arrived on campus, I got in the habit of eating a bagel with a cheese spread or jelly for breakfast. We attended classes, conducted research in the library, viewed films, and went on field trips. We did not have televisions in our apartments. We toured California's Central Valley. During one field trip we heard Maria Varela, one of Starry's colleagues, speak at a university. She was a land rights activist and she had been a SNCC field worker and photographer. She served as our instructor on grant writing. She told us she had worked with sheep herders in a village in New Mexico.

During our field trips, we visited housing cooperatives, farming sites, attended meetings, and visited the homes of farm worker advocates. At one house, we heard horrible stories about the life of farm workers. Some farm workers said they lived in small living quarters, worked long hours, and experienced a lot of domestic violence. I thought their stories sounded like modern day sharecropping. My grandfather Moses Meredith and his first wife Barbara Nash Meredith left their share cropping housing, purchased a farm, and started a new life in rural Attala County, Mississippi in 1923.

One day we went to San Francisco and ate at a restaurant in the tourist district. We even passed by San Quentin Prison. Whenever Nancy or Mike took my picture they would say, "Will," and laugh at me because I gave them a beautiful smile when I heard his name. I talked about him often. Our distance made my feelings for him grow stronger. Nancy said, "Will must be some kind of fellow." On our walks to campus, Mike taught us Spanish words. Believe it or not, I still remember the cursing words. We shared bits and pieces of our history with one another as we walked to and from campus.

We were required to read a book about each other's culture. I bought and cracked open "Black Elk Speaks."

Black Elk described Indian life differently than Cowboy and Indian movies. Black Elk recalled, "We are children of one mother and their father is one Spirit... Now I light the pipe, and after I have offered it to the powers that are one Power, and sent forth a voice to them, we shall smoke together.[i]" We attended a Pow Wow (Indian ceremonial dance) in Davis, California too. I gained a new perspective. Their struggle was not much different from mine.

I learned that Mike came from a large family who migrated to Texas from Mexico. Mike became a County Commissioner. He transitioned a few years ago. Nancy is a member of an Indian tribe in Montana. Residents of the Flathead Reservation facilitated an annual POW WOW reenacting the Lewis and Clark expedition encounter with the native people. Today, Nancy and her family own a ranch which tourists frequent. I am Black from the south. I was born in Los Angeles and raised in Mississippi. My father's family in northern Alabama are descendants of the Cherokee tribe and my mother's side from Central Mississippi descend from the Choctaws. In Davis, I learned new information about my Indian heritage.

Will had Choctaw blood too. His Aunt Dorothy and Uncle Ronnie had deep Indian features. Will, a dark-skinned man, has wavy hair. Will's grandmother Christine Easterling McGee was from D'Lo, Simpson County, Mississippi and so was my grandfather Joseph James Coleman. My great grandmother Cora McDonald Coleman was from the Welch's Plantation.

During slavery, the Welch's Plantation held many slaves in bondage. Will and I and my friend Brenda visited Dickie Selman in D'Lo once and Dickie told Will and I the descendants of the Welch's Plantation still owned businesses in Simpson County, Mississippi. Will and I used to tell people our grandparents were from D'Lo. Sometimes people would say, "What! Ya'll might be related." We would both look at each other and laugh.

My cousin Fran attended our graduation ceremony at UC Davis on June 14, 1998. The four of us obtained certificates of completion from the Rural Development Leadership Network. Afterward, I spent the night in Sacramento, California with Fran, and her teenage children. I stayed up late watching VCR movies because I had not watched any movies or watched television the entire time I was in Davis. I glimpsed at the news in passing once at a restaurant.

Fran asked me, "You still up."

"Yah," I replied. I was helping myself to VCR movies.

One of the most memorable sites we visited was Allensworth, California, a settlement established by a former slave. It had once been a self-sufficient town which the railroad ran through. It is now an historical state park. I wrote my cousin Ronnie who was born and raised in Los Angeles and told him about the park. He told me he had never heard that a former slave started a settlement in any part of California. Seems like information about Allensworth should have reached the history books for school age children. Come to think of it, I don't recall reading about Mount Bayou, Mississippi during school either. Mount Bayou was an independent town founded by former slaves. The most famous of them was Isaiah T. Montgomery.

When I returned home June 16, 1998, Will and Traa were at the airport to pick me up. Will told me Traa said, "There go

Miss Mary when he spotted me getting off the plane."

They were both glad to see me. Will was happier. We had been talking 128 days and we were totally in love. We were moving so fast. Big Will told me his son had never been in trouble and he was going to be good to me. Big Will had great things to say about Will. I had never heard any man speak so highly of his son. Everyone called him Big Will and they called Will - Lil Will. I believed his father to be telling me the truth. So far, so good. We got back into our routine.

We were so in love; our love for one another was magical. One day, Will locked everyone out of the house. When I came outside to get in my car, I passed by four people sitting on the porch. Everyone spoke; but they had expressions on their faces. Some nights, whenever we had a moment, Will turned on the music and we danced in the living room at 2504. Our love for one another was like good weather. The passion between Will and me was an active flame engulfing every inch of our existence. We went back and forth from each other's houses. We talked on the phone when we weren't together. He popped up at my house. I popped up at his house.

Will and I attended a Banquet at Tougaloo College honoring Geronimo Pratt. We heard him speak before the Banquet and Will took a picture of me with Geronimo Pratt and his wife. Most students took pictures with him only. I felt it was more respectful to take a picture with the couple. I felt especially happy to meet Geronimo Pratt. I read about him in the book about Huey Newton. Tupac Shakur mentioned him in one of his songs. Tupac had said in an interview that he visited Geronimo in prison. Tupac's mother Afeni Shakur was mentioned in Newton's book too.

I watched the OJ Simpson Trial, and it was interesting to read later that Johnnie L. Cochran Jr. said he wanted to win the OJ Simpson verdict so he could free Geronimo Pratt. Cochran and Pratt were from Louisiana. On my 37th birthday July 20, 2000, Will handed me a copy of *Last Man Standing: The Tragedy and Triumph of Geronimo Pratt*. This 500-page book was one of the best books I'd ever read about a social justice leader. My cousin Ronald entered California's prison system from LA as a juvenile offender in 1981. He recalled being in San Quentin with Pratt. Pratt said when he went to prison in California there were only single cells. Pratt was against double celling.

In late June of 1998, a Vista Volunteer at work Mrs. Albert Brown told me about Kids College at Jackson State University and I paid $35 down and enrolled Traa in Kid's College. When he graduated from Kid's College, Mrs. Brown was in attendance because her granddaughter graduated from that class too. I was out-of-town and couldn't attend. Will attended. Traa learned how to use the mouse on the computer during Summer Camp and I purchased educational games, and he started using my desktop computer on Dewitt.

My sister Evalyn purchased Traa workbooks which included Alphabet and word tracing and coloring activities for the summer. She told me Traa would have to be prepared for kindergarten at home. As Traa traced his alphabet in the workbook, I discovered he learned how to write Z and another letter better. His handwriting improved and his vocabulary increased. He loved the computer games I purchased at Sam's. He would play the games for hours. He played a farm game repeatedly and learned the names of farm animals and loved catching eggs on the computer.

During the 4th of July weekend Will and I went to New Orleans to attend Jazz Fest. I had picked up a coupon book and we found a nice hotel near the French Quarter, which is several square miles downtown frequented by tourists from around the world. Will and I enjoyed strolling through the French Quarters browsing t-shirt shops, restaurants, and other venues. New Orleans is one of the most romantic cities in the south.

At Jazz Fest, we looked at the line up and walked around trying to determine which acts we wanted to see. Will decided to go to a payphone to call Big Will. Will asked his dad which group on the lineup at Jazz Fest was good. Big Will told Will to call out the names of the groups. Will called out the names of jazz vocalists; then, he called out "Etta James." Big Will suggested we attend Etta James performance, and we did.

I was familiar with Billie Holiday, Nancy Wilson, Ella Fitzgerald, and Sarah Vaughn, but I wasn't familiar with the music of Etta James. When we walked to her stage a crowd of people were standing around. On stage was a thick, high yellow, older lady seated on a stool. An older man in the crowd was talking to people standing in front of us; he said, "Etta James was made like a coca cola bottle back in the day!" Will and I looked at each other; we kept listening. The older gentleman had plenty to say about Etta James. After we got back home, I ordered one of her CDs and Will and I listened to it. We fell in love with "At Last." Her entire album was good.

Soon, we talked about moving in with each other. His house was like a family house. I was troubled that Harry was murdered off Gordon Street near my house. Deputies secured his corpse at the funeral home. The losses were back-to-back. Will and I started talking about buying a house and starting over. Well, I am a serious person. So, I called a realtor the following Monday and told him we were looking for 4 bedrooms with 2 full baths. Traa was a little grown person and offered to go with me to look at houses.

The realtor gave me the address of a house on Woody Dr. and a house on Dorgan St. We visited those houses, but I didn't have any connection to them. My Aunt Judy told me when I saw the right house, I would know immediately I was in the right place. Eventually, we drove up to a house on Maria Court which had four bedrooms, two full baths, a beautiful fireplace made with large bricks, a large back yard, and a large master bedroom on the opposite end of the house from the other bedrooms on a lot nearly ¾ of an acre. I knew I was standing in the right place. I told Will about the house, and we drove there the next day to look at it. When the three of us pulled in the driveway in late July, Traa asked, "Whose house is this?"

I replied, "I hope it will be our house one day."

Traa questioned my statement and asked, "Our house?"

Will seemed a little apprehensive about the house at first. He said we will have to put a lot of money into this house. He said we would have to remove the old carpet and buy new carpet and paint. Then, the next day he was more positive and approving. I packed my dishes and belongings in boxes on Dewitt Ave. and gave Will the key. The house closing was August 10, 1998. That Saturday, August 15, 1998, Will, Tyrone, and his friends moved our belongings in the house. I was out-of-town in Epes, Alabama for the

Federation of Southern Cooperatives Annual Meeting which is always on the third Saturday in August. Before it turned dark, I drove to the house on Maria Court. I couldn't get in because Will and his friends were in between driving loads of our belonging from Newport St. and Dewitt Ave. and the door was locked.

I walked to the house next door to use the phone and met Henry Hendrix. He was very nice and let me sit in his kitchen until Will returned. I felt proud because Will's friends complimented us on our new home. They put up his bed. Will and I cleaned up the large master bedroom and bath, put sheets on the bed and slept in his bed that night. We slept in that bed together in our bedroom for 22 years and 10 months. We changed out the box spring and the mattress again in May of 2020.

Will's ex-wife had enrolled Traa in Dawson Elementary School during pre-enrollment of 1998. I drove to her apartment in North Jackson and got Traa's birth certificate so Will could enroll Traa in Kindergarten at Wilkins Elementary School near our new home. Will started working at McCarthy Holman at night. I got Traa ready for school. I watched Traa walk pass three houses to get to the bus stop each morning. He was the youngest child on the street. Traa was five; the boy next door, Hendrix, was six; Brice was eight and Tameka and Chas were six and seven. The children on the street became very close. They used to sit in the middle of the street with their legs crossed like Indians and talk for hours.

My Aunt Mary gave us a rug as a housewarming gift. She said, "You got a house here. Don't listen to people and get into debt buying furniture. Pay the mortgage on time. Fix and paint one room at a time." Aunt Judy came by; she said,

"I told you. You knew - didn't you?" She complimented me and Will and walked through the house. She teased me and Will about having fun by the fireplace. We smiled and did not reply.

After Thanksgiving that year, Will decorated the outside of our home. He purchased a Christmas tree. We decorated the tree with ornaments and candy canes. Traa made a Christmas ornament with a toy red apple at school. He put his name and 1998 on the apple and his ornament was placed on the tree for the next 20 years. This Christmas ritual was new to me because I used to put up a Christmas wreath on Dewitt Ave. But I hadn't had a tree up since my dad left the Summer, I turned 12.

Will mowed our lawn and took great care of it. Our yard was beautiful. He kept the hedges trimmed and the yard up. He washed the cars and cleaned the inside and outside of the windows. I had a blue 1996 Toyota Camry and Will was driving a yellow 1979 dodge. He loved it. His grandparents purchased his first car, a brown Duster, in high school.

In six months, Will and I went from slow dancing in a hole in the wall to keeping house and living together. That January, we threw a 60th birthday party for mama, Hazel Hall. Our family and friends attended. My sister Evalyn and her husband Bill and the children attended. Odessa and Tip Light, Tyrone, my god brother Andrew, Mrs. Liddell, Sandra, Gladys, Mudd, Charles and others attended.

We celebrated our first dating anniversary, February 8, 1999. Will brought me flowers, a teddy bear, a pair of gold hoop earrings, and balloons. I purchased several shirts and wrote him a card expressing my love for him. When he got off work late at night and returned home, he would find a love note taped on our bedroom door. He often told me, "I'm the luckiest man in the world."

We were both showing each other a side of love that was different and so exciting. Will was the first man beside my boyfriend Ricky from Pensacola to be faithful to me. Will and I both had holes in our hearts from heartbreak and infidelity. A song writer once asked, "How do you mend a broken heart?" The process is different for everyone. I was the healing power for Will; he was my healing power.

Will loved every inch of my being because I belonged to him and no one else. I loved every inch of his being because he belonged to me and no one else. Loyalty, faithfulness, and devotion are not always mutual, and when it's present - it's heavenly – it's magical. Will and Meredith's love lasted.

Will and I showed our love for each other every day through our actions; our love grew deeper and deeper. His Aunt Chris told me one day, "Mama would have loved you because you love Lil Will." His other Aunt Pinkie D. (Little Sister) told me the same thing years later. His Aunt Dorothy made the same statement after Will's death. I took their statements as the highest compliments because Will was raised by his grandmother and everyone in his family always told stories about Christine McGee (mama).

Above our bed is a large, framed portrait of a boy and a girl at an ice cream parlor. She is wearing a peach bonnet, and he is sporting a brown felt hat adorned with a beige ribbon. A glass of milkshake is between them on a small round table containing two straws - one for him and one for her. She is sipping, enjoying the milkshake. He is smiling, looking in her eyes rather than partaking in the milkshake.

He is happy to see her happy. The point the painter makes is evident. The peace in her eyes is more valuable to him at that moment in time than the sweet savory taste of ice milk. Brown is one of Will's favorite colors.

Sometimes Will passed me the straw; sometimes I passed him the straw. That's how love is. Pleasing is in the hands of the pleaser just as beauty is in the eyes of the beholder. Will told me he hung the painting above our bed because the painting represented us when we were children.

Pretty soon, I questioned Will about his intention to marry me. We were shacking up and playing house quite eventfully. I knew Will loved me. I certainly understood the deepness of my love for him. I was helping Will raise his one and only son. I attended most of Traa's award programs because I had a salaried position by then with a flexible work schedule. I could attend Traa's school programs. I was proud of Traa. He would smile when he saw me in the audience. His teachers noticed me too. He was excelling academically. We paid Ma Mae to pick Traa up from school the first few months of kindergarten.

One day, Ma Mae told me Traa picked four or five wildflowers from her front yard and gave them to her. She said he said, "Here, you can have them. This is my love for Miss Mary."

Ma Mae told me she said, "Thank you You're so sweet." It's true fathers teach their sons in positive and negative ways how to treat women.

I got laid off from the Mississippi Association of Cooperatives before Christmas of 1998. I started collecting unemployment and Will had to foot the bills primarily by himself. Our wedding fund was not taking off so well. Will paid the mortgage on time every month. He was devoted to his small family – Meredith and Dew. He called Traa 'Dew' which was his grandfather Leeandrew's nickname. Will never called his son Traa. But most people including me accepted the nickname Traa's mother gave him. Uncle Butch, Maurice, and a few other family members called Traa "Dew." Boobie's daughter Carmon, who was younger called Traa "Dookie."

A few months later, Starry Kruger came to Jackson to meet funders at the Foundation for the Midsouth on Pearl Street, and I met her downtown for lunch. She was interested in me getting back into her program. She drove me in a rented car to Voice of Calvary Ministries which was in a two-story house on Saint Charles Street in West Jackson to meet with CJ Jones who was over the Development Department. CJ had participated in her program in the late 1980s. I knew CJ too. He and Melbah Smith and Ben Burkett of MAC were friends.

Midway through our informal meeting, Starry was engaged in a discussion about a potential job for me. I was stunned – happily so. I didn't know we were going to discuss my employment. CJ said there was a data entry job available in his department which paid an hourly wage. Mrs. Lee Harper was the president of the nonprofit and a week or so later she hired me. Starry was so pleased because she wanted me to get back into her program so I could complete my masters degree through Rural Development Leadership Development. I needed a field project at a nonprofit to get back into her program. My field project with MAC was a farmer's market on the outskirts of Holly Springs, Mississippi. Eventually, Lee Harper resigned.

Elizabeth Perkins, daughter of John Perkins, was my co-worker. She directed Voice of Calvary Ministries after school program. I enrolled Traa in the program. Traa needed health insurance, so Donna Pollard, in accounting, had Traa's health insurance deducted from my payroll check. Will and I set a wedding date for Saturday, September 25, 1999. Phill Reed became the president of Voice of Calvary. CJ took a position heading MACE in Greenwood, Mississippi in the Mississippi Delta. Alexis Spenser-Byers took CJ's spot in the Development Department. I was moved up from a data entry clerk to Assistant Director of Development when Alexis stepped down to move back to California. Alexis fought hard to increase my pay in my new salaried position. We had a special friendship; she owned a home nearby and she even used Will as her plumber.

Pastor Govan and his wife Helen Govan were associated with the ministry, and they met Will and Traa. They offered to counsel us since we were engaged. Our wedding plans were on the prayer list at work. The Govans were great counselors and eventually they became our friends. Every morning our staff prayed. One morning I announced a boy from another street ran Traa home and I made him go back outside and defend himself. The other boy's mother sent him out and came out too. Sam said, "Oh boy let's pray for Meredith, she is going to be in the streets fighting instead of keeping peace." My parenting concepts were not acceptable to everyone. In the end, my influence wasn't as bad as my coworker had predicted, Traa and the other boy became good friends.

Traa and I use to throw pennies, nickels, and dimes on the wall. He started getting pretty good and was collecting change. His mother came one day to pick him up for the weekend. I told her Traa was getting good at pitching coins on the wall. She criticized me for teaching him how to gamble and I told her, "Well if you don't like my parenting style, get your son and raise yourself." She seemed surprised by my response.

I should have been surprised by "it," but I felt like pitching pennies was a skill rather than gambling. Ha Ha. Will didn't cry about it either.

Mr. Govan told Will the Mississippi Construction Education Foundation had a program which trained men and paid for them to obtain skilled trades. Will tried to enter the Electrical Journeyman Program but he told me he didn't feel welcome in their program. So, he went to South Central Heating and Plumbing, and he obtained a better vibe there. Shawn, the youngest son of the owner of the multimillion-dollar business helped Will walk through the process. The hourly wages were low, but he was working; his education was funded.

Will's schoolwork was interesting and sometimes I read his lessons with him. He read about ancient aqueducts – water systems. The Aztecs had water canals in Mexico City; the ancient Egyptians, the Greece and the Romans built aqueducts too. Will was making As and Bs in school; he was learning on the job and earning money on the side.

His first plumbing job on the side was a re-piping job for Ms. Okolo. Will underpriced the job and his childhood friend Rick helped. It took them three or four days to complete the job. Anyway, he was getting his feet wet and learning as he went. The Saturday before our wedding my 17-year-old cousin Jessica and her 18-year-old boyfriend Justin got married in our den. She was expecting their first child which they named Janae. Her wedding reception was at a wedding hall on Capitol Street near Prentiss Street. She called me after she and Justin settled in and told me, "Being married is different from dating someone. I know. I'm married."

I was amazed by her revelation because she was 17 and explained to me what to expect because I was getting married the following Saturday. During the days leading to our wedding, Will's Aunt Chris purchased his white suit and Traa's white suit. She agreed to cook and to bake Will's chocolate cake; mama was almost finished with my wedding dress. Ma Mae had encouraged mama to make me a special dress. Mama warned me, "You better not gain no weight. This dress is measured to fit you."

"I ain't gaining no weight," I replied. By then, mama was hand stitching pearls on the front of my dress. It was beautiful. Mama tailored the dress to compliment my shape. Will was planning his bachelor's party. For some reason no one planned me a bachelorette's party. My grandmother Beulah arrived on the 21st of September. She started washing and cleaning. She even ironed Will's shirts and was sharing laundry tips with me. Will was impressed because my grandmother was old school. She put extra touches on things. Mrs. Liddell told me, "If you start fixing his plate, you'll be fixing his plate for the rest of your lives together."

The day before our wedding my grandmother kicked Will out of the house. She told him, "You can't stay here tonight. That will bring bad luck to your marriage." Will packed up his clothes including his white suit, white shoes, and lavender tie and went to stay at Sparky's and Sheila's house in Presidential Hills. While he was enjoying his bachelor's party, I was at home with Traa, my grandmother, and other visitors.

On our wedding day I was so nervous, my younger sister Jozzlyn helped me get dressed. Ma Mae put on my make up. Rev. Booker did not show up to marry us. Someone shared the bad news with me and that made my anxiety worse. Will recruited Mr. Govan to perform the ceremony. Mr. Govan and Mrs. Govan had counseled us for months. He had offered to perform the ceremony, but Will had asked his pastor first. I liked their counseling style because they worked as a team, and they were very practical.

In July, I attended New Galilea Church with Will. That Sunday, Traa attended church with his mother. Will and I went to Rev. Booker's office after church. Will introduced me to him and he agreed to come to our house and marry us on September 25, 1999. He forgot and begged Will's pardon later.

Mr. Govan married us. Will and I jumped the broom, and I remember our family and friends were noisy and cheered when we jumped the broom; we backed up from the broom and trotted and jumped the broom. We were so happy. Will just held my hand and wouldn't let it go until the photographer Frank Taylor started taking pictures of us and group pictures with our sides of the family.

We did not get to eat our wedding food. By the time we decided to eat, everyone had eaten, many of the entries were gone, and people had packed up plates. We cut our three-tier white cake and his chocolate cake and toasted to champagne. Our plan was to go to New Orleans that Sunday. We had a room at the Holiday Inn on Highway 80 Saturday night where Will's friend Dwight worked. Our wedding song was "At Last" by Etta James. We had grown to appreciate her music after seeing her at Jazz Fest the previous summer.

Our wedding was 25 minutes late. During that time, Will borrowed Mr. Govan to marry us, he borrowed his Uncle Fred to replace Spanky as the best man, he borrowed Uncle Fred's wedding ring and my mother's ring to place on our fingers. Will returned Uncle Fred's ring and mama's ring. We opened our wedding gifts. We had wine glasses, dishes, expensive cookware, gold plated utensils, bowls, etc. We sat around and talked. Will's stepmother Betty came and talked with my dad, stepmother, and grandmother. I placed my diamond and rubies ring on my wedding finger. Will's wedding finger was bare. We grabbed our luggage and we headed to the Holiday Inn.

As Will and I walked in the Holiday Inn holding hands, wearing our wedding attire, we passed by a crowd of

Jackson State University students. Someone announced, "Look at the newlyweds." Hundreds of students stood and clapped loudly as we walked past them. It was captivating. I blushed as we walked by the students lined against the wall waiting outside a banquet room. We were thankful to God we obtained enough cash in our wedding cards to go to New Orleans that Sunday. We spent our first night together as a married couple at the Holiday Inn on Hwy. 80. It was the beginning of our amazing life together.

Turned out Jessica was right; being married is different from dating. I experienced intimate freedom. Our honeymoon was exciting. We enjoyed each other and our time alone. After we returned home, I fell right into the tradition of southern women. Will was traditional too. He insisted on taking out the garbage and doing the manly things. I stuck with the traditional female household roles. I picked up a few things from his Aunt Chris too. In her household the teenage girls cooked and ironed. One Sunday, me, Will, and Traa visited Voice of Calvary Church. Pastor Phill Reed preached; in his sermon, he suggested parents give chores to children when they are young because good, work ethics at home follow children into adulthood.

I gave Traa the task of raking the leaves around the Magnolia Tree in our front yard when he was in the 1st grade. The girls two houses down, Chas and Tameka always helped him rake the leaves whenever they saw him working in the yard. By second grade, I taught Traa how to iron. Some of my co-workers criticized me and said I was a lazy parent to have a 2nd grader ironing. My sister Eva's children had chores. Will's Aunt Chris ran an efficient household; everyone had chores. Her teenage girls Mary and Annette could cook and clean like women. The oldest girls ironed clothes for the entire upcoming week. In her household, preparation was essential. She was old school.

During my two years at VOCM, I traveled with Sam Pollard to obtain a grassroots leadership training at Mary Reynolds Babcock Foundation in Winston-Salem, North Carolina. When we returned from North Carolina, I wrote a grant to the foundation, and we obtained funding, and I organized the *Grassroots Leadership Institute*. VOCM rented space at the Holiday Inn on Hwy 80 for the Institute.

Somewhere along the way we believe the grass is greener in another yard. I left Voice of Calvary Ministries VOCM and accepted a job as a Community Organizing at Southern Echo in January of 2000. Soon, Will completed four semesters at Hinds Community College.

Then Will accepted a job in the City's Water and Sewer department as a supervisor. There were many complaints about his pay being higher than existing workers, and Will decided to look for another job. Turns out he was earning more than workers who have been working for the City of Jackson 10 years or more. The pay system gave two percent pay increases which did not keep up with inflation. The pay system was set up during Jim Crow. Go figure!

Harvey Johnson was the first black mayor in Jackson. Will recalled that the workers were all looking forward to the new mayor coming to speak to them. When he came to greet them, he did not take the time to listen to any of their grievances and he left. Will said the workers wanted to tell him that the pay scale system was not lifting black men up but was keeping a knee on their pockets. Will said morale was low and he didn't want to work for the city anymore. Employees assumed a black leader would change the old pay structure. But it didn't happen.

Will heard Jackson State University had a plumbing department. He applied there and obtained a salaried job which was his highest earning job in his career. James McGrew was working in the department when Will arrived. He and James became fast friends. They created a plumbing enterprise business together. Will did commercial plumbing at South Central Heating and Plumbing. Will had learned the art of ordering supplies from Bobby Ainsworth.

Will was learning residential plumbing. McGrew did residential plumbing. Together Will and James were a powerful team. They purchased machinery and tools and took on residential and commercial jobs on the weekends and during the evenings. Some evenings Will made it home after 8pm. The Department of Facilities Management at Jackson State University presented William (Plumber) the Employee of the Month plague in Feb. of 2003.

I was excited about my Community Organizer position with Southern Echo in Jan. of 2001. The salary was a little higher than VOCM. Echo offered a 401 K, and health insurance. Southern Echo had obtained grant funds to train communities to challenge redistricting maps at the local, county, and state level. The Honorable Henry Kirksey learned demography and map drawing during WWII. He was one of the first black senators in Mississippi in the 20th century. He taught Mr. Hollis and Mike Sayer, both former SNCC organizers, demography mapping and they taught us. Southern Echo had been instrumental in paving the way for blacks to get elected in more offices by challenging the redistricting process after the 1990 census. I was one of four employees hired to challenge the 2000 redistricting process at the community level in Mississippi, Alabama, Tennessee, and South Carolina.

At that time, Derrick Johnson was a lead redistricting trainer for Southern Echo. The first time I went out of town, Will dropped me off and put my luggage in the trunk. Derrick was driving and Mr. Hollis was on the front seat. I sat in the back seat alone. Derrick looked at Will and said, "We will take care of her man." Will said, "Okay," then he walked off. Derrick and Mr. Hollis were teaching community groups how to draw political districts which made it possible for black candidates to get elected. They were teaching demographic concepts like stacking, cracking, and packing in the confines of voter suppression.

We travelled to different meetings in different states. Sometimes there were 20 people in the audience; other times there were 80. Derrick was a lawyer, and his training style was to inform and engage. Mr. Hollis was very engaging. He started his trainings with questions. He once jogged up the aisle in a conference room in South Carolina at the beginning of a training. His stunt was a huge attention grab on the audience. He was in his sixties; he was famous. He was adored.

At some point Derrick had some irreconcilable issues with management and he resigned. Aaron Hodge, one of the four hired the day I was hired, and I started traveling with Mr. Hollis and eventually we travelled to communities without Mr. Hollis. Hodge was a former agricultural specialist in Epes, Alabama for the Federation of Southern Cooperatives, the parent company of the Mississippi Association of Cooperatives.

By 2001, Mike Sayer was teaching us to draw demography maps on the computer. I mastered computer mapping.

Sometimes, Will and Traa attended meetings with us in Mississippi. Will was working at the Ameristar Casino when I was training at a hotel in Greenville. For a few days, he stayed in the hotel with me and got up early and drove to Vicksburg.

I sided with Mr. Hollis at work which was extremely costly. Aside from siding with his faction, I had been informed that we could take grievances to the Board of Directors. I presented a grievance to the Board. One of Mr. Hollis's friends was very disrespectful to me. He was rude and loud. I was crying when I got home. Believe it not, Will had never seen me cry before. He asked me what the board members name was. He looked his name up in the phone book and he and his friend Sam went to his house off Jayne Ave in West Jackson.

Will said he knocked on the door and walked in and stood in his living room with his hands in his pocket. Will told the board member his wife Meredith came home crying. Will told me he yelled a line from the Malcolm X movie, "Get your hands out your pockets!" Will said he assured him he was unarmed and showed him the loose change in his pocket. Will said they talked it out. Will wanted the board member, who was a black male over 60 years old, to know he didn't think it was fair for him to talk rude to his wife. Will said he told him, "You wouldn't want anyone to do your wife like that." Anyway, Will left in peace. Apparently, freedom of speech ain't free.

Unfortunately, by November of 2003, I experienced another life change. I got laid off from work again. The first time I got laid off, we had just purchased a home. This time I had purchased a new 2001 Nissan Maxima. I was collecting unemployment again. Will had the burden of the car note, the mortgage and us. Will paid those bills on time.

Getting laid off twice changed my mind about working in social services, and about working with my own race. I found in the nonprofit scheme of things - nepotism, favoritism, mess, funding issues, or late payroll checks put a bitter taste on the entire idea of helping. Really, helping! The internal issues at Southern Echo were funky. In the end, I thanked them for sending me on my way 30 days before our 401 K vested, and 10 months after purchasing a car which had been used to take voters to the polls to help elect the first black female alderman in Drew, Mississippi. Hollis, Mike, Leroy, and Brenda laid off four of us in one day. They were courteous. They hated to see us go due to lack of funding. The real issue was probably politically more akin to founder v. funding. They had their positions, votes, and power. I had Will. Thank you. No further statements.

Many nights Will and I sat on our porch and enjoyed the cool night air. For a few years an owl perched on the light pole in the left corner of our front yard near Unc's driveway. Will loved nature and he knew everything about the galaxy and the stars. We would walk in the driveway while he pointed out the big dipper (seven bright stars) or the little dipper (seven bright stars) and the brightest star is Polaris the North star. During slavery times, Africans studied the stars to find the North star to walk North. Will had been under his grandfather's thumb when he was a boy and learned a lot from him about animals, nature, and life.

One day I went to work with Will. He was doing a plumbing job for Uncle J-Boy on Eastview Street. Will complained that I was on the phone too long and wasn't there trying to learn how to fix the sink or pass the tools;

so, I quit and never tried to go to a work site with him again.

I never knew how much money Will made because he dealt in cash. I paid the household bills, typed all the plumbing invoices and receipts, and put money in our investment club account; soon we became vested partners in Heirs United Investment Club. The funds doubled every seven years. Through it all, we've both had life changes. Life is a roller coaster. Believe that. We learned to put one foot in front of the other and keep moving.

After being laid off, I was in my last semester at Antioch University McGregor (known now as Antioch University Midwest). Then, I started writing my four-chapter capstone project "Characteristics and Strategies of Successful Small Business Leaders." My faculty advisor was Virginia Paget, PhD. I was enrolled in the Individualized Degree Program which the school has since discontinued. Students wrote their own degree curricula and were able to use nine to 12 credit hours of our field work toward advanced degrees. My field project was developing a set of manual demographic maps which I completed under Mr. Hollis' direction on the job. Ophelia Kelley, my childhood piano teacher, and Brenda Hyde, Southern Echo, were on my degree committee.

I told my former co-worker Myra who worked at MAC that I didn't plan to work for anyone else anymore and I was thinking about starting a business. Myra suggested I start a typing and writing service because I was a good writer. Mama had an old business plan for a typing service. She gave me the business plan folder. I studied the plan and started attending training sessions at Jackson State University's Small Business Development Center. Larry

Ward served as my business counselor.

I wrote my business plan narrative for Typing Solutions Resumes & Wills. I changed the word 'wills' to etc. My former co-worker, Bobby, a paralegal at Owens and Owens, suggested I change the name and he explained state law had limitations for the development of legal documents. Larry Ward and the other counselors didn't write business plan narratives, but they prepared the financial statements such as the breakeven analysis and the profit and loss statements. Since Mr. Ward saw I had writing skills he started giving me referrals to write business plan narratives for his clients. Writing and resumes was more lucrative than general typing, so I promoted my writing services and paid to be listed in the phone book. Will supported my decision to start a business but he asked me if I planned to use my master's degree several times.

In many ways, I was using all the skills at my deposal to run my new business. I was editing research papers, drafting bylaws, personnel rules, etc. I learned modern style rules for APA when I was working on my master's degree. My paralegal training was very valuable too. My capstone project was the first time in my life I wrote four chapters. I collected raw data and conducted scholarly research. My manuscript was 63 pages. I was relieved to complete my master's degree in Rural Community Development & Public Policy. I was looking up.

CHAPTER 2
Every Inch

Well, Will was stacking up cash so we could take a vacation after my second layoff. Will lined up plumbing jobs and we headed to Las Vegas to see Big Will, Deloris, Moony, Poncho, and their children. Mama rode with us and stayed at Cousin Marjorie's house. Will was the main driver. I had my business plan folder and was reading research for my new business venture. We were so excited when we drove through Hoover Dam. Will, Traa, and I got out of the car and took pictures. It took us 32 hours to get to Vegas. We did not even stop to get a hotel room. Mama insisted we keep moving. She reminded us that years ago when they travelled west, black people couldn't get hotel rooms, they pulled over, took naps, and kept driving. Anyway, it was uncomfortable.

We drove by Moony's house first. Traa stayed with Moony and her four children. They were a few years older than him. They knew him and they had stayed with us too. I remember once, Will had Adrene, Avion, and Kenny cut our yard. Adrene and Avion are Moony's boys and Kenny is Poncho's son. Kenny started limping pretending he had hurt his leg and couldn't help mow the yard. It was so funny. I mean, it seems like it took more energy to pretend he had been injured than it did to help. Adrene wanted to get him too. The girls Deasia and Akasia were sweet. They had a little cat fight. I broke it up and everything was cool. Mooney's children went back to Vegas. We got to see Kenny more. He stayed in Mississippi with Ola Mae and with Poncho for a while. Eventually, Will was able to get Kenny to do plumbing jobs to earn a little money. He was a character! Kenny told me often I looked like his mother. She was Hispanic and the apple of his eye.

We drove mama to Cousin Marjorie's house. Will and I stayed at his dad and Deloris's apartment in North Las

Vegas. Will was glad to see his sister and her children. I met Moony once on Newport Street. Big Will was smiling from ear to ear. He offered us everything from coffee, cheese, crackers, cookies, and food.

I was ready to see the strip. I had never been to Las Vegas, neither had Will. He had always wanted to go to Vegas because his sister Moony and brother Poncho lived in Vegas. Moony took us on the strip and we walked through Caesar's Palace, Circus Circus, and MGM. Everyone had exotic pets snakes, lizards... Will and I looked at those glass cages. A couple times the cage was behind our heads.

We waited all day to do something, but nobody gathered to move until at least 10 pm. We were in a different world. We enjoyed ourselves and we spent one day and our final night at Cousin Marjorie's house. We spent time with her children on the last night. Mama had them to herself the entire week. On the way back, Will's finances were a little low. I think gambling ate the linings in one of his pockets. He denied it!

Anyway, we drove back to Mississippi as quickly as we had left. When I got back, I started my business, Typing Solutions Résumés & Etc which was classified as a data entry company. I did not pay sales taxes like I had when I had a convenience store. There is a difference between retail and service businesses. The customer base for my convenience store was driven from walk-in traffic, price, location, and customer service. In my service business there was no walk-in traffic. All clients came from ads, referrals, word of mouth, and promotions.

I took out a newspaper ad with *The Mississippi Link,* but I didn't run the ad long and I didn't get much out of it. I went to my local library – the Richard Wright Library on McDonald Rd. and asked Debra, the head librarian, to let me hang a flyer on the bulletin board. She allowed me to hang the flyer on the bulletin board because library patrons came in frequently seeking typing and printing services.

It took me 30 days to get my first customer from the flyer at the library. My first client was a white male student taking a correspondence course through the mail. I typed his Civil War report on the use of submarines by the Confederacy. Within a few years, I had a steady flow of general typing and printing services. I did graduation cards, business cards, résumés, cover letters, flyers, invoices, letters, and I typed legal documents 'as is.' My flyer stayed on the bulletin board for over eight years. Flyers produced more new business than any of the ads.

An employee at the Eudora Welty Library sent me referrals too. Larry Ward sent me referrals to write business plan narratives. I wrote a business plan for a School of Barbering in Magee, Mississippi. I wrote the business plan narrative for TCL Financial and Tax Services. I also wrote the business plan for Community Students Learning Center in Lexington, Mississippi and I wrote other plans. I started picking up college students too. Will posted my flyers around campus at JSU. I obtained new business from my listing in the telephone book. I was listed under "Typing," but I thought I would be more visible being listed under "Resumes." Eventually, the Internet replaced phone book ads. I rented a Xerox and started doing funeral program booklets. I taught myself how to create picture collages by looking at funeral program designs.

My capstone project was approved, and I was slated to walk across the stage to get my master's degree in Rural

Community Development & Public Policy at the auditorium in Dayton, Ohio on July 18, 2004. Will, Traa, Khadiya, and I went to Dayton for my special day. After I obtained my degree, I walked through the crowd and found them and when we got on the elevator, Khadiya took my cap off my head and put it on her head. She was the daughter I never had. She loved us – her family. She started calling him Uncle Will when she turned four-years-old. She and Traa were close. Every year, she taped pictures of her mother, Willa, her siblings, Joss and Calla and Will, Traa, and I in the front of her school folder.

Will was injured on his job that year. His shoulder dislocated. He had a surgery performed by Dr. Berry Mun. He put a pin in Will's shoulder, and it stopped coming out of place. He injured his arm while lifting furniture all those years. One of his friends, Carlos, injured his back when he moved furniture for a company on Capitol Street in downtown Jackson. I learned that the occupation of black men is sometimes hazardous to their health. Will's arm came out of place one day when he was playing basketball at Dwight's house. Sometimes he would put it back in place by himself. I took him to the ER four of five times so the nurses could relocate his shoulder. I felt his pain.

Will told me his grandmother warned him he would not be able to do physical work. When he was a boy, he had braces on his legs like the movie character 'Forest Gump.' Will told me his Uncle Butch asked his mother to take the braces off Will's legs. She did and Will said he was so relieved. He chose to do physical work. I think manual labor seemed natural to Will. When I met him, he was as strong as an ox. He had a six pack. He was muscular and fine. He was the apple of my eye no matter what. I remained his for the rest of his life and beyond. I remain his to this day.

When he turned 42, he was diagnosed with JOBS Syndrome. There are 250 people in the USA with JOBS like Job in the Bible. The life expectancy is 38. Doctors use to tell Will he was a walking miracle. People with JOBS have compromised immune systems and are attacked with infections. At first, he was plagued with boils and staph infections. As the years passed, the infections became more serious. Will got Osteomyelitis in the bone of his right ankle. His infectious disease doctor discovered the bone infection via an x-ray, and we rushed with him through the halls of UMMC hospital to set up an emergency surgery.

We met with the surgeon who told us that they would have to cut one inch of his bone out to keep the infection from spreading. We were told that the bone would merge into his ankle, but he would more than likely walk with a limp. For six months Will had a halo on his leg, he had to walk with crutches, and he was confined to a wheelchair. The medical team had their plan and predictions. Will had me. I was his backbone.

Will told me no one could have ever told him he would be down at 42. It was hard. After he built up his strength, he made it a habit to hop to the car or his truck and go somewhere. He wouldn't lay down. If he drove to the convenience store one of the younger guys would go in the store for him. Somedays, Will would get calls for plumbing and McGrew would go on the job with him and treat him just like he did when he was standing up. McGrew use to call Will, "Lil Homie," but McGrew treated Will like a blood brother.

People play different roles in people's lives. Will had

relatives and he had many brothers and sisters who were not blood related to him. People visited, people brought cards, brought cash, and brought food. Rev. Boyd and his prayer warriors prayed with Will. His Aunt Dorothy always prayed with him.

Will's bone merged into his angle one inch, and he did not walk with a limp. Will was so happy to be walking again, but he had pain where the rods from the halo had been especially when he walked long distances. Will opened a business called "Maintenance Masters" and he poured his energy into plumbing. Sometimes he worked under Johnny Young's license. I'm not sure how Will met Mr. Young, but they had a great relationship. Will continued to work with McGrew. Will was hard at it. Sometimes there would be four men on the back of his F-150. Will's motto was *make it look cute*. McGrew still worked at JSU in the plumbing department, but he joined them on the weekends.

One day the hard drive on two of my computers went out. I told Will, "I'm out of business. My computers died." I was upset. I had work on my desk I needed to complete.

Will said, "Let's go and buy another one."

"Really," I said.

"What you think? You think I'm out here playing around or something?" He asked.

"No, I lied."

This may sound strange, but I was stunned. Will drove around in an old truck, wore work clothes all the time, and wore blue jumpsuits in the winter. Besides a super bowl party, a barbeque, a birthday, or trip out of town, all Will did was work. I didn't expect him to have enough cash to buy me a new computer from Office Depot. We drove to Office Depot, and he purchased me a new computer – top of the line. I came home, set the computer up in my home office, and kept working.

Will was a Ford man. We paid $2,500.00 for Will's first F-150. The motor went out in Will's truck; so, he was looking for another one. Tip Light told Will about a F-150 truck. One day Will told me, "I need you to help me buy a truck."

I said, "Okay, how much you need?"

He said, "I have $200.00. I need $100.00." He didn't really need my help to buy the truck. He wanted me to see the truck. He usually involved me in financial matters. Will bought it. He loved it.

In 2006, RDLN was having an Assembly in North Georgia. I told Will I was planning to go to the Georgia Baptist Conference Center in Norman Park, Georgia, and he told me he wanted to go too. I called Starry and asked her how much room and board and meals would be at the conference center. I think she said $1,000.00 for 4 days and 3 nights. She asked me how I planned to get there. I told her I planned to drive. At the last hour, there were issues getting a flight to the conference for Unita Blackwell; she was on the board of directors of RDLN. Starry called me with a proposition for Will and me to drive to Mayersville, Mississippi and pick up Ms. Unita Blackwell, let her spend the night with us and drive to north Georgia that next morning so we could arrive for dinner to eat with the Assembly group. For our services, the cost of Will's room and board was adjusted.

Will completed his plumbing jobs and got his money up and we were ready to go. Either Odessa came to stay with Traa, or he stayed at his friend Dejon's house one block away so he could attend school. Will drove us past Vicksburg to Mayersville. We parked in Ms. Unita's driveway. She was smiling when we knocked on the door and we went in to help her get her luggage in the car. We had to pass by her Walk of Fame to reach her bedroom where her luggage was. We had to stop and take it all in. There were pictures of Ms. Unita at the White House in the Oval Room with President Jimmy Carter and President Gerald Ford. There were dozens of pictures lined up in her hallway displaying her life of activism.

Ms. Unita had a charismatic and charming personality. She was 6'3, dark, commanding, and regal. Will asked her about the pictures. She told him that she had travelled to China and different foreign countries normalizing relations for presidents and that she was a MacArthur Genius. She was a great storyteller. We were willing listeners. We never turned on the radio. We listened to her storytelling for hours on end. She started telling us about West Helena, Arkansas, her mother Verdie, her father, and her schoolteacher who told her mother to change her name from the initials UZ to Unita. Ms. Unita said her teacher told her mother to name her "Unita" because she was gonna' be somebody one day. Oh my God. That teacher had great vision.

A few days before our trip, mama gave me and Will a new bed frame for our guest room. When Ms. Unita arrived, mama and Dorothy Stewart, the founder of Women for Progress, came by, picked up Ms. Unita, and took her to a restaurant. I didn't go with them. They just took my company. I stayed at home and packed and got ready for our road trip. It took us eight hours to get from our house in south Jackson to Norman Park, Georgia. Ms. Unita was so humble. She mentioned how nice everyone was at the restaurant and how nice my breakfast tasted. She started the storytelling again.

Ms. Unita told us how SNCC workers visited Mayersville and invited the church goers to help register voters so black people would have a better life. She told us she told her husband, Jeremiah, she was getting involved with those young folks. She said he told her they would stand up together at church. In other words, Mr. Jeremiah was not going to let her stand alone and leave him seated. She said the day they stood up in church was the day she got involved in the movement and became a SNCC organizer.

It was amazing to me because I met Mr. Jeremiah in 1995 while working for MAC on Hamilton Street in downtown Jackson. Whenever he came to Jackson he stopped by the office and spoke to everyone, especially Melbah M. Smith and Ben Burkett. He used to update us on his wife's travels. He used to say, "Unita is here..." I wondered who his wife was. He spoke about his wife who I assumed was an important woman. One day Melbah told me his wife was Unita Blackwell - the first black female woman elected in 1976 as mayor of a town in the State of Mississippi.

I called my sister who lived in Morrow, Georgia and we met her at a Chinese restaurant for dinner. We enjoyed our meals. Eva, Ms. Unita, Will and I took pictures by the small waterfall as we were leaving the restaurant. Ms. Unita enjoyed us and acted as if she had known us all her life. Ms. Unita and Charles Sherrod, husband of Shirley Sherrod were the most famous people at the conference; once we arrived at Norman Park, Georgia, we did not get to talk to Ms. Unita until she got back in the car with us for the drive back to Mississippi. Will was enjoying himself, hanging out conversing with different conference attendees. We enjoyed ourselves. Good times.

Honorable Unita Blackwell, left, Meredith center, Will, right

Will's next health episode was horrific. He and the guys did a commercial plumbing job, and he developed a fugus on his lungs which created a cavity which opened and bled slowly. He was the only person under that building who caught a fugus. His immune system was too weak, perhaps for his profession. I went with him to the hospital. He had to have IV antibiotics for eight weeks; he was advised to stop smoking cigarettes and he did. We travelled to Atlanta for the Meredith Family Reunion which was organized by my sister Eva. I packed his medicine and had to give him his antibiotics intravenously twice a day. I was his caregiver again. I gave him his meds, took his blood pressure, and made sure he went to his doctor appointments.

He stopped doing plumbing work under houses and buildings. By now, Will was taking breathing treatments for his lungs regularly at home. He was being monitored closely by his doctors. He had a regular doctor, a lung doctor, and an infectious disease doctor. He saw specialists from time to time too. We were learning more and more about the JOBS Syndrome. Before we knew it, Will bounced back, gained weight, and appeared extremely healthy. His doctors gave him antibiotics and we tried remedies to build his immune system. Will looked healthy and he told me he felt healthy.

Will had a period of good health. He worked, we travelled, we celebrated our birthdays, holidays, and our anniversaries. Will barbequed in the spring and fall and Labor Day and Memorial Day. We hosted New Year's Eve parties every year. Every year we cooked and different people bought dishes and good cheer. The children fired fireworks. No one at our house ever shot guns in the air. Thank God because every year people across the country die from celebratory shooting. I wish this news was discussed more. You know, as the saying goes, "A bullet don't have no name on it." Morgue employees tag names of innocent victims of stray bullets too much. Celebratory shooting used to be associated with the 4th of July and New Year's. Now, people shoot in the air any time of the day or night. The world has changed. Our communities have returned to the rise of senseless killings.

New Year's Eve 2017 the den. Will and Baby James kneeling
Standing mother and daughter on the end
Center Jessica, Meredith, and Jameria

Buck, Khadiya, Will, Jessie, Meredith - New Year's Eve 2017
Photos William and Meredith McGee Family Collection

In 2008, after Senator Barrack Obama advanced ahead of Senator Hillary Clinton, Will and I were having a rough time financially. He had experienced multiple bouts with JOBS. He had to take IV antibiotics again and his health had declined. He had closed his business and applied for Social Security and been denied three times. He obtained a lawyer. He was in the hospital for several weeks and ended up at Select Specialty Hospital for Rehabilitation. He had died and had to be revived. I cried like a baby peeking through the ambulance window watching the drivers pump his chest. I wanted to be near Will and squeezed in the hospital bed with him which became a ritual.

One day a doctor came in and jokingly asked, "Which one of ya'll is the patient?" Will laughed and said, "I am." We loved every inch of each other.

53

Rev. Boyd of Pearl Street A.M.E. Church and several prayer warriors visited Will. From time to time, Rev. Boyd had hired Will for plumbing. Ms. Earnestine, Jeffery, Poncho, Lisa, his son, and others visited Will. The rural fellows sent messages to Will. I read the messages to him. He was so sick and so frail. I smiled and remained upbeat, but on the inside, I was crying and screaming. Will's body was traumatized again.

God was with Will. We prayed. He prayed. His Aunt Dorothy called as always and prayed with him. In time, he became stronger. He picked up the pieces, put one foot in front of the other, got out the bed, and made some moves. He refused to lay in bed all day. He found a way to be productive. When he couldn't go under the house. He found someone who could. When he couldn't stand in a ditch and connect fixtures, he found someone who could. When he couldn't hold a wrench. He found someone who could. When he couldn't walk through Lowes, he rode through it.

When he needed legs, someone became his legs. When he needed a driver, he found a driver. When he couldn't pick up the parts, he called parts in and had the parts and supplies delivered. When he exhausted his options, he sent referrals. He made amendments and adjustments in life. But he never stopped trying to do what he did best. He used his skills. He trained dozens of men. He employed dozens of men. I thought his profession was counterproductive to his health, but I had never considered that idleness would be worse. There are two sides to every story. If someone tells you one side of a story and you don't have the other side, you won't have enough information to form an honest opinion.

Meredith & Will at a restaurant in May 2016.

Will was kindhearted and helpful; he loved the elderly, especially those in Shady Oaks; he helped whenever and however he could. He was blessed and highly favored. Yes indeed. He had struggles. He walked through pain daily. Sometimes, he had the right team of doctors. For a decade, his pain was managed. There were years when his pain was not managed. Over the counter pain pills caused other problems to his stomach. There is a catch two phrase in every situation. Regardless of his imperfect reality, Will got up every day, put on his shoes and found a way to be productive. He enjoyed life, his wife, his family, and his friends. He was the oldest of 15 or 16 children. Plus, he had dozens of siblings by other mothers. He never had a lonely day on this earth.

He was a man. He was a hardworking man. He was big bro. He was adored. He was sometimes misjudged. Sometimes his kindness was rewarded. He always remembered his grandfather Leeandrew's words, "Live to see another day." His grandfather told him, "I'll come get you if you are defending yourself, but I'm not coming if you take something." Will recalled that his grandmother Christine told him, "Ain't no such thing as a fair fight." She also told him he would not be able to do manual labor. He couldn't accept her vision for him. Every man he knew performed manual work. His father was a painter. His grandfather was a pipefitter, a farmer, and a carpenter. His cousins were brick masons.

Will often proclaimed, "I wasn't raised by no dummies." He was telling the truth. Leeandrew modeled wealth. He and his siblings were landowners. Their land was on the outskirts of Canton near their place of birth. Leeandrew was a homeowner, a member of Progressive Baptist Church, a mentor, a good neighbor, and he had three or four sources of income. Leeandrew had a job. He operated a livestock enterprise in the county where he raised hogs and other livestock in a stall. He sold and had hogs butchered. He raised chickens too. Sometimes, chickens ran freely in his backyard on Newport Street. Not everyone understood the value of walking in the backyard to get eggs for breakfast. Production v. consumerism. Will said sometimes his classmates teased him about the chickens running freely in the yard.

Leeandrew and Christine loved gospel music. The Canton Spirituals, The Soul Stirrers, and other musicians use to practice in the living room at 2504. Leeandrew and Christine attended gospel shows at different churches. Will and other family members loved gospel too. Leeandrew dressed well and had his felt hats custom made on Farish Street at Dennis Brothers. Will had his felt hats custom made too. His fitted baseball caps were size 6 7/8." His Aunt Dorothy told him often, "Boy you just like daddy."

He was. One evening, Will and I were on our way out, and Khadiya noted, "Uncle Will has swagger." He, a Stacy Adams man, was stepping like black men do when they know they look good. Dressing well was a custom of the McGee men.

During the Pandemic, I drove past a vacant white building on or off Hooker Street several times as we left Stamp Burgers so we could look at his surname – McGee – at the top of the white building. Leeandrew and Christine ran a Cleaners business there. Leeandrew and Christine ran a café too. Their first home was in the Dixon. Then, they moved near Lanier H.S. and before Will was born August 28, 1965, they purchased their home at 2504 Newport Street. Will's Great Aunt Edna, the youngest of the McGees, born in 1922, lived on Morton Ave. in Georgetown. She told Will and me she use to walk to Shady Oaks to prepare food for Dew (Leeandrew) and Christine if they were sick.

Aunt Edna's generation was only two generations removed from Slavery. Their generation exemplified the African village concept. Spouse first, then family, then neighbor, then race. If a fight broke out any adult could give correction. If the adult swatted the child's behind, the child's behind got swatted again when he or she reached home. Edna's home was full of pictures. She had a large Plantation picture in her living room. She pointed to a toddler sitting on the ground and said, "This Dew." The massive picture was Museum worthy. Leeandrew and his siblings purchased their own land together not far from that Plantation. Yes, they did.

Aunt Edna had a framed picture of Dew's boy Will and his second wife Meredith on her wall. Christel McGee Wilson proudly gave her a framed picture of us at our garden wedding, and Edna hung it high. Christel was one of Will's first family customers. She told him, "Charge us like you would charge anybody. You got a family to feed." Christel and Little Dot, an adopted child of Leeandrew and Christine, paid Will fairly. Little Dot would say, "Boy" to Will's price before she went in her purse.

Edna was the last living child. She allowed me to make copies of her pictures such as Sara Travis McGee, her mother, Chester McGee, her brother whose nickname was Crack; he owned farmland in Illinois. She let me make copies of her family funeral programs which included her siblings, and her nephews. Somehow her family line - the Flemings- were related to the owners of Slaughter Funeral Home located on the Southside of Chicago. The Slaughters were from Canton too.

During middle school at Brinkley, Will discovered that girls and his male friends enjoyed visits to the hog pen. Few young people in Will's generation had the opportunity to hear a pig snort, see an animal slaughtered, see sausage produced, or see a horse eating hay. Will learned the value of stashing cash from his grandfather. Leeandrew provided for three generations. He fed his children and his grandchildren. Neighborhood people stopped by and ate too. Christine cooked in big pots. They had plenty. Will said she use to say, "Cook enough for company."

Odessa and Little Sister would take over my kitchen when they stayed over two or three days. They used to cry laughing at my little pots. Will told me, "I'm use to your cooking." He enjoyed my cooking. As the years passed, I learned to cook larger portions. I lived alone for nine years of my adult life. I cooked best in small pots.

Will loved his grandmother's style of cornbread. Michelle and Christy cooked like Mrs. Christine. Christel cooked well like her mother. She worked for Jackson Public Schools as a head cook. She cooked cakes from scratch and chicken tetrazzini to die for. Michelle, her daughter Cristy, Big Dot, Karen, and others can burn too. Big Dot (Dorothy), Leeandrew's baby girl, makes cakes from scratch too.

Will's grandma had never heard of the JOBS Syndrome, but she envisioned that Will would be better off using his brain than his hands. She had placed him in a shoebox in her dresser draw near her bed when he was a few weeks old; he was sickly, and she nursed him to good health. She had taken him to the doctor and given the doctor permission to put braces on his legs when he was four years old. She talked to the doctors about his skin, his bones, his rashes, and his ailments. She talked to the white doctors, the black ones, the tall ones, the short ones, the old ones, and the young ones. She raised her 9th son's first born. She and her husband adopted her 9th son's first born and others. They were village leaders.

Will kept the memory of his grandparents going. He discussed them and the old days with anyone willing to talk about it. Many remembered. Many called Mrs. Christine McGee "mama." She was always mothering and protecting. Will never forgot any of his childhood. "I had a great childhood," he recalled. He spoke fondly about his travels to Chicago, to Georgia, and to Brooklyn, New York. Will enjoyed life. He lived each day with a purpose. He loved deeply. He loved me with a feeling.

Will and I were excited when I received an invitation to speak at the 15th Annual Booker T Washington Economic Development Summit, September 15-17, 2010, in Tuskegee, Alabama. The theme was "Revitalizing Entrepreneurship and Procurement Opportunities in Small Towns and Rural Communities." This was my first paid speech. Alice Paris, my former co-worker at the Federation of Southern Cooperatives put my name on the table after hearing me talk about Heirs United Investment Club at the Women's Conference hosted by Mississippi Association of Cooperatives the previous year in Vicksburg, Mississippi. Will joined Heirs United Investment Club in August of 1998. Will and I were vested partners in this General Partnership. Alice was a rural fellow. I had attended her graduation ceremony in Concan, Texas in 1997.

Will and I rented a car and Will drove us to Tuskegee. He loved driving and we both enjoyed road trips and touring historical sites. We toured the Tuskegee Museum on campus, and we took pictures around campus of statutes and historical markers. It was exciting seeing exhibits on Booker T. Washington and the students. We toured the Tuskegee Airmen exhibit off campus. During our visit we learned that Tom Joyner, radio personality; Lionel Richie, singer, and Ralph Ellison, famous author, attended Tuskegee.

George Washington Carver headed the School of Agriculture. Carver arrived at Tuskegee Institute in 1896; after his arrival Carver developed over 300 uses for peanuts and over 100 uses of the sweet potato. He invented lotions, dyes, and soaps. Carver sought to develop products which would economically benefit black farmers in Alabama's

Blackbelt, which fueled the agricultural economy during and after slavery. This dark soil was naturally rich; slaves were transported to the Black Belt in great numbers where productivity was great and profit for planters was high.

Carver worked with the white and famous inventor Thomas Edison. Edison was faring well economically; but Carver wanted to uplift the rural black farmers who were living in persistent poverty. Carver obtained three patents, while Edison obtained over 1,000 USA patents. Edison invented among other items the light bulb, the phonograph, and the motion picture camera. Carver invented flour, laxatives, cooking oil, paper, stains, dyes, paints, writing ink, vinegar... Unlike Edison, Carver had been enslaved and it was important for him to lift his brothers and sisters. Today, the Black Belt region is plagued with high poverty, substandard education, high unemployment, weak infrastructure, and limited health care.

Will was proud of my presentation on the 17th. The main story was how 11 family members and one family friend formed Heirs United Investment Club with a collective deposit of $800.00 in 1997 and within 10 years our assets (investment in mutual funds, direct stock, and cash) exceeded $40,000. Members' funds (vested partners in particular) had doubled in the first eight years. I founded and conceived the idea to start the investment club. But I was financially illiterate at the time. Since the company was formed, I learned from those at the table who understood the stock market. I applied myself through self-study too.

I went from zero understanding to becoming the Financial Partner who picks funds for the Investment Club influenced in part by research conducted by the membership. Will accepted his first assignment to conduct research of the large stock segment in 2002. He researched a S&P 500 Index fund. He called T Rowe Price Family of Funds and asked the representative to give him the price of the mutual fund going back five years. The representative gave Will random prices of the fund over the previous five years. The S&P 500 Index fund includes large companies like AT&T, McDonalds, Walmart, MGM Resorts International, Carnival, Best Buy, Gap, Home Depot, Target, AutoZone, etc.

After Will researched the stock, Heirs United purchased shares of a S&P 500 mutual fund at $43 per share. The next month the price per share declined to $33 per share. So, we purchased additional shares at the lower price and held on. This process is called "Buy and Hold." Some investors "Buy and Sell." Our investment group memberships peaked at 26. Today, we have 25 members; we've always invested conservatively. However, there is always a risk when a group invests in the stock market. Diversification is key. Most of our holdings have been in mutual funds, some direct stock, and then savings.

I also told the audience how I stood in one line depositing or withdrawing funds from me and Will's checking account, while my stepson stood in another line in the 2nd grade to deposit $5 at a time in his saving account at M&F Bank (now Renasant) in Clinton, Mississippi. Traa also receipted customers for Will and my businesses. At that age, he knew the name and every tool on the back of Will's truck. Traa set up my office technology too. We purchased a stock option of McDonalds stock for Traa once he saved $100.00. He chose McDonalds because he was a fan of Happy Meals. Traa wrote checks to pay our bills in the 4th through the 8th grade. Either Will or I signed the checks. The point was parents can teach children financial literacy and business practices when they are young.

On September 16, 2010, I accepted the Booker T. Economic Summit Award on behalf of Heirs United Investment Club. Others accepting awards represented University departments with multimillion dollar budgets. I was honored to speak on behalf of a small family run financial venture. Afterward, people in the audience told me they were impressed that our family was investing together. The Kennedys (real estate – alcohol, entertainment), the Rockefellers (banking), and other families collectively built dynasties in this country. Today, the mass media appeals to our race a desire to consume. We're brainwashed to believe our consumption of goods and services is a status of wealth. In reality, our spending creates wealth for business owners.

Will told me, "You knocked em' out."

I thought about Mr. Blake who was proudly one of Will's early plumbing customers. Mr. Blake used to tell Will, "You're my horse even if you never win a race." Someone is in your corner when they say that. When it comes to true friendship, it's show and tell. People show us by their actions who they are.

That October, Will and I travelled to the Louisiana Community Coalition in Hammond, Louisiana which was a quick ride for us - less than three hours. Will developed deeper relations with some RDLN rural leaders like Ben, Mily, Leticia, Carol, NKwanda, Michelle and Twila during that trip. Twila was a former Tribal Chief of the Band of Chippewa Indians in North Dakota. She nicknamed Will "Wild Bill." When I heard her call Will "Wild Bill" I wondered what Will did to get that nickname. However, the nickname was a compliment. He loved it.

Will wanted to visit their reservation. She invited us. She spoke with a dominant presence. Will didn't say much but he was paying attention to the story telling. The stories were rich. Will said, "Twila stands like a boss." Over time, my friends became Will's friends and Will's friends became my friends. Me and Will had relations with rural fellows outside of the Assemblies which convened every two years.

One year Leticia traveled to Vicksburg to attend a wedding. She informed me and Will of her arrival date; we drove to Vicksburg to hang out with Leticia. We had a great time with Leticia at the Bottleneck Bar at Ameristar Casino. Leticia immigrated to America when she was a teenager. She told us she and her brother walked in part through a tunnel to cross from Mexico to America. She is now a USA citizen.

After another episode with JOBS, the sun shined on our house in 2011, Will finally got a Social Security check in the mail. Traa obtained a check for a few months. Once he turned 18, the checks discontinued. It's a shame, it takes going to the brink of death for someone to get Social Security even though it's their money. Will was happy his Social Security kicked in, but he always said, "This ain't no money." I didn't care about the money, I just wanted Will to live long. Staying at the hospital with Will became part of our routine.

Sometimes the doctors and healthcare staff had no problem distinguishing which one of us was the patient because Will had tubes hanging, a blood pressure cup on his arm, and three of four IV drips. He told me one or two times to move over, but he never wanted me to sleep on the couch. My devotion comforted Will. I saw a twinkle in his eyes, felt love from his touch, and calm when he held my hand.

We fell in love with each other over and over again. I was his wife, his caregiver, his healthcare broker, his heart, and his inspiration. He was my husband, my provider, my lover man, and my inspiration. He placed me in his heart next to his grandmother. He told me she told him, "Give me my flowers while I'm living."

Will planted me flowers on Mother's Day because I helped him raise his son and because I reminded him of his grandmother – Christine – the special woman who raised him. He bought me flowers. He showered me with gifts. I showered him with gifts. He tried to give me everything I wanted. I tried to give him everything I thought he wanted. I thanked his grandmother many times. I never met her personally, but I knew her stories. Will talked. I listened. I talked. Will listened. He was a loving husband, a great father, a great son, a wonderful big brother, a devoted nephew, and a decent man.

My office was my woman cave. His man cave was our bedroom and the porch. If he was having a private conversation he walked on the porch. He preferred to have his cell phone on speaker phone. Will's hands were his plows; he had arthritis in his joints and holding a phone was not a part of his routine.

I reinvented myself into an author toward the end of 2011 and co-founded a publishing company with Darlene Collier called Mose Dantzler Press. We published her memoir "Married to Sin," and it was translated into Spanish by the brother of a rural fellow Mily with the Rural Development Leadership Network. Anyway, Will was so proud of me and Ms. Darlene. He was front and center at our book events.

Will invited Aunt Rose and his younger sister Karen to our book event December 10, 2011, from 2:30 to 4:30 pm at the Medgar Evers Library on Medgar Evers Blvd. They attended. Will was pleased when people attended my book events. Sam and Boobie attended several events in 2012.

Will had four different month-long hospital stays. On one occasion, He had been misdiagnosed on the previous hospital visit and given a C-pack of antibiotics and cough syrup. His friend Rick, his cousin Maurice and brother Poncho had to come to our house to help me get him in the car. I returned to the hospital with him. I walked outside the ER to call Traa and Big Will.

Will screamed my name so much, the nurse came outside and found me. Will later told me he felt he would die if he didn't see me. The ER doctor told me Will's vital organs were failing. I gave them approval in person to perform surgery on Will. They rushed Will into surgery to save his leg and his life. The surgeons removed the muscles in Will's right leg to save his leg. Will's body was so traumatized by the surgery; he had to learn how to hold a spoon and eat and walk again.

That time Will stepped in water which gave him the flesh-eating infection (Fasciitis) which was eating his muscles. He had stopped going under houses and now his weak immune system was posing a new threat to his capacity to perform his livelihood. I wanted him to give up his trade for good. I made my position known. But habits are hard to break.

Will admired couples he saw walking and holding hands. Will use to say, "Now that's love there. They are walking, holding hands, and happy." I told my sister once, "I'll live in a shack with Will." Thank God we never had to live in a shack, but we went through our share of financial hardships.

At Select Hospital, I realized how important aides are. Will lost weight. His weight had fallen to 98 pounds. I had to drive my stepson to school every morning in Ridgeland and the aides delivered cold food to Will's room. They didn't try to help him eat. When I came into the room to see if he had eaten, he told me his food was cold and no one helped him. I would go and get him something to eat and drink. I met with the hospital administration the following morning and asked them if they could give him cold cereal and toast for breakfast. They tried that. He started gaining weight little by little and building his strength. Eventually, his physical therapist helped him walk up the hall to rebuild strength in his legs.

The hospital administration offered to arrange for Will to continue rehabilitation so he could have around-the-clock nursing services, but we agreed he would be better off at home. I knew the routine. They gave him a PICC line, and I administered his meds and IV antibiotics at home. He got on the Medicaid Waiver program in 2012, and they sent him home aides. Unlike the nursing aides at Select Hospital, the home aides had more compassion for Will. He picked up weight and reached 136 pounds. His skin was dark brown; he told me he felt good. His skin appeared darker when he was sick.

Once Will was admitted into UMMC for a few days and one of his former home aides saw him. She yelled, "Mr. McGee." Then, she ran to him and broke his neck off hugging him. She was one of the great nursing aides. She kept Will's room clean, sanitized the doorknobs, refrigerator handles to free his area of germs.

Not enough aides understand the significance of sanitation. The good book says, "Cleanliness is next to godliness." Cold, flu, and other diseases spread through the fingers. These days restaurants and retail establishments have become increasingly lax on sanitation. Will and I went to a McDonalds restaurant in Belzoni one year and saw dead flies on the counter. I asked an employee if I could see a manager and a young black women appeared at the register.

I asked, "Did you know there are dead flies on the counter?" She appeared alarmed by my news and requested an employee clean the counter. I didn't buy anything; but I couldn't leave without saying something. Will and I have eaten at fast food restaurants in Yazoo City, Indianola and other areas in the Mississippi Delta and received great service. That day was an exception to the norm.

During his senior year in high school, Traa totaled Will's F-150 truck when he hit a pole on I-220 coming from school at Saint Andrews Ridgeland campus one night. Traa was blessed. He walked out of the truck without a scratch. He called home and Big Will answered and Traa told his grandfather that he needed to speak to his daddy or his mama. Will was not home so Big Will gave me the phone.

Traa said, "Ma I tore the truck up."

I asked, "Are you okay."

He said, "Yes." I told him okay. I'll call Will. I asked him what happened, and he told me he stayed up late with his classmates when they went on their college fieldtrip, and he fell asleep at the wheel.

Maybe Traa assumed we would be upset that he wrecked the truck. The truck is a resource but not as valuable as his life. Vehicles can be replaced but lives cannot be replaced. Will called a towing company on Medgar Evers and he told Will, "Your son is lucky, but your truck is gone." Will didn't have a truck which put a dent on getting work done.

That Summer, our nest became empty. Traa accepted a Presidential Scholarship to attend Jackson State University in Jackson instead of the scholarship at Millsaps College. He was persuaded to accept the scholarship at JSU by Tyrone Hendrix who grew up next door. Tyrone obtained his bachelors and masters from JSU. He was a proud JSU alumni. Tyrone's father Henry is our unc' and neighbor.

That summer, Traa fell in love with a girl from Cleveland, Ohio. She graduated in May of 2016 - the year Michelle Obama delivered a Commencement Speech. His girlfriend left first, and he followed her that October and he has been in Ohio since. Will and I talked to him as he drove by himself through Memphis, through Nashville, through Kentucky and on the route Will and I had taken to travel north since he was in Elementary school.

- - - - - -

Let me tell you, privacy is heaven. The lyrics of a song by the Ohio Players noted, "Heaven must be like this. Heaven is you," Sugar Foot sang. Heaven is being able to walk through your house anyway you want to. We had the living room, the kitchen, the den, the fireplace, the front yard, the back yard, our bedroom, and guest bedroom (Traa's old room) to ourselves. We didn't even have to close our bedroom door. Freedom is an empty nest!

"Meredith" Will yelled. "Come here." If I didn't hear him, he walked to my home office and sat in that green chair or stood at the door.

Will often said, "I don't play second base." He didn't care if I was in the middle of a thought or paragraph or inserting a picture. What he needed me to see on television was always urgent. "You gone miss it."

On March 21, 2013, Praeger Publisher published *James Meredith: Warrior and the America that created him,"* a biography I wrote on my uncle. I obtained the rights in my contract to have 50 rare leatherbound books printed. Will and I paid the extra cost for printing. Book collectors across the country gave me praise for owning rare books on a renowned Civil Rights icon. We sold the books for $250.00 when we could. That same year, I opened Meredith Etc, a small press in February of 2013, and published "Odyssey" a collection of my poems, writings, and the study I wrote on Small Business Leadership as credit toward my master's degree.

Late in mid-February Will got sick and ended up in the hospital for three weeks. I was planning to speak that March at CSW 57 at the United Nations Commission on the Status of Women at the UN Church Center in Manhattan across from the street United Nations. Normally, I would fly to NYC. But Will, mama, and Ms. Virgie wanted to go with me. Will, mama, and Ms. Virgie obtained clearance to enter the United Nation compound and to attend the Women's conference. We rode to Buffalo, NY in mama's SUV to visit my Grandmother Beulah for several days. Then, Ms. Virgie drove us to NYC. Ms. Virgie drove the entire trip from Memphis to NY. When we checked into the hotel, two blocks from Times Square, we discovered we would have to pay for parking to the tune of $48.00 each day.

We settled in the room; a few minutes later Will decided to walk to the lobby. I walked with him. We had our coats, scarves, and hats. It started sleeting. I suggested we go back to the room because it was sleeting. We were in NYC. It could snow. Anything could happen. Will was still recovering from another episode with JOBS.

Will said, "I'm in NYC, I ain't staying in no hotel." I was thinking to myself. His physical therapist was walking him up the hallway at our house the previous week complimenting Will on his progress. Here we were, in Manhattan, NY walking through the crowd while it was sleeting, taking pictures, and acting like tourists. Will is an amazing man. He was excited. He walked and I walked.

By the time we made it to Times Square, we went in McDonalds to get something warm to drink. We used the restrooms and Will lost his scarf. I was concerned he lost his scarf because I wanted his neck covered. I am the caregiver for crying out loud. We went back to McDonalds. As busy as it was, Will walked up to the counter and told a cashier he had left his scarf and an employee handed Will his scarf which was a sign of good fortune. Will had walked for blocks and Will was as happy as he could be. He hadn't complained about pain or being tired. He was enjoying the moment.

That night he discussed getting up early so we could walk to the Today Show and get on national television. The next morning, we didn't get up early enough to walk to Times Square to the Today Show. Will was disappointed but he was ready to see the city. We went to the United Nations to get our conference badges. We stood in a long line with women from around the world. Some had on African attire, Asian attire, etc. The employees took our pictures and gave us our blue name tags on a silver beaded chain.

Below our photos were the words, "CSW 57, March 15, 2013." Will and I toured the United Nation exhibits and took pictures. The exhibits include pictures of human experiences from every corner of the world. Will and I share a love for history, culture, music, and art.

Then, we walked across the street to the UN Church Center where Starry was hosting a book event for Shirley Sherrod, the wife of Charles Sherrod, a former SNCC organizer from Albany, Georgia. By then, Shirley was famous. She became a household name after she was wrongfully fired as the first Black Georgia State Director of Rural Development for the US Department of Agriculture during the Obama Administration due to a controversial news report by Breitbart News which was led by a right-ring blogger.

Shirley was forced to resign and later offered a different job which she declined. She was offered a book deal with Simon & Shuster and the result was her memoir *The Courage to Hope*.

I told Will and Ms. Virgie I was introducing Shirley, and I didn't have a prepared presentation. I was sitting in my chair trying to figure out in words a starting point. Will videoed my presentation and took pictures. He was not involved in social media. He usually shared his videos and pictures with his friends and relatives Carlos, Short, Ladarius, Ant, Spanky, Karon, etc. I'm thankful I was able to preserve the videos from his phone on our website and to our social media sites.

I remember saying, "Shirley Sherrod was one of my mentors and one of the big wheels at the Federation of Southern Cooperatives."

Under the leadership of **Starry Kruger** everyone had to be ready to serve, ready to speak, ready to drive, ready to carry... Will and Ms. Virgie thought my presentation was good. I was relieved. There were local and federal elected officials in the room plus us waiting to get autographed copies of her book. Will and I took a picture with Charles and Shirley Sherrod. Every day our large party broke bread together at different restaurants.

Ms. Virgie drove us sightseeing to Harlem. When we reached the Apollo Theater she parked the car, and Will and I walked around. Mama and Ms. Virgie stayed in the car. There were book and retail vendors along the street and a line of people auditioning for the Lion King play. Mississippi has short street blocks but blocks in Harlem are long. People were in long lines stretching blocks as far as the eye could see.

After we talked to a few street vendors, we looked at the line. Oh my God the line was long. Hundreds of beautiful Black sisters and brothers were lined up. The expressions of the faces we passed looked like the faces you see at a family reunion. Everyone was so happy and excited and ready to get a part in the Lion King play.

Will said, "We can't go to the end of that line."

I said, "We can't cut in front of all these people and go in there." Will started walking. I walked with him. We J-walked from the side of a book vendor's stand and walked past the crowd; we smiled and walked in the Apollo. I had a poster of my Uncle J-Boy (James Meredith) in a round container. My uncle had allowed mama to produce the poster a few years earlier. An artist at a maxima security prison in Atmore, AL drew the artwork. Uncle J-Boy kept the original art on canvas with his museum collection on Griffith St. Will saw that famous wood stump and he pressed his hands across it, and he said, "Take my picture." We took a few pictures. Then we walked in the theater. Someone asked if we were there to audition.

Will stated, "We want to donate a poster of Civil Rights leader James Meredith to the Apollo Theater."

She said, "Okay. I'll get someone."

The attendant or volunteer went to tell someone we wanted to make a donation to the theater. Shortly afterward, someone arrived. We made introductions and he led us down the hall to his office and I pulled out the poster. He said he knew of James Meredith, and he would be honored to pass the poster to another person who could accept the poster and hang it up. We thanked him and we walked to the car and told Ms. Virgie and mama about our tour. Will told mama a worker was happy to accept her poster of her big brother which also displayed an image of her mother Roxie and Father Cap. Mama was pleased.

Ms. Virgie drove us to the Cotton Club. An employee allowed us to go in for a quick tour. About three people were in the building. We admired the pictures on the wall. "Harlem Nights" and "Life" were two of Will's favorite movies. Will and I were big fans of Eddie Murphy, Richard Pryor, Redd Fox, and Charlie Murphy. We watched "Life" dozens of times. We walked out of the Cotton Club, got in the car, and Ms. Virgie drove us across the bridge. We admired the water and headed back to Manhattan where we noticed a series of Trump towers beaming in the NYC skyline.

Ms. Virgie was the captain of the ship. She was interested in us enjoying our road trip. Next, we attended the UN Status of Women's marketplace in Manhattan. I sat up my books and mama's poster of my uncle at a table. Will sat beside me. Two women walked to the table and started telling us what they knew about James Meredith. The women were wearing traditional African attire. One of them was from France. Will was impressed that an African French lady knew so much about Uncle J-Boy.

I manned my table and Will started walking around, looking at the various product offerings from women who lived around the globe. Someone invited him to attend a session on Human Trafficking where he remained for over an hour.

For one hour Will heard the sinister stories of survivors, victims, and advocates of Human Trafficking which he learned was really, modern-day slavery. Poor girls were pushed from poverty into the system of Human Trafficking every day. He learned girls 10 or so were forced into prostitution by the droves, 10's of thousands were forced to be sex slaves annually, in Pakistan, India, and other countries in the Middle East. Will told me one male advocate couldn't reveal his name because he was on a powerful sex trafficking profiteer's hitlist.

Will told me when he was in his 20s, he attended a house party and several males he knew were planning to run a train on a teenage girl and he helped her get out the house. His moral consciousness opposed the rape and torture of women. I remember my older brother Bobby telling me he took a lick and passed one to save a teenage girl in our neighborhood in the late-1970s.

Will told me the organizers of the event said government officials turned their heads to this profitable and immoral business. Oh, Americans can't judge other countries. American victims were present too. You mean a Spanish speaking woman escaped forced labor in The Land of the Free? Yes. Unfortunately, teenagers of every ethnicity are sex trafficked in every corner of the USA. How do men and leaders get to a point where getting one's rocks off and profit is more valuable than human dignity and freedom of a women - as Tupac spit, "men come from a woman."

The disturbing stories Will took in that day were more profound than a Hollywood movie.

RDLN members and friends attended a play and musical called "The Total Bent" which was Will's first and my second time attending a Broadway play in NYC. We enjoyed it. On the way back home, Ms. Virgie drove us past the White House. Will and I ate at My Three Sons restaurant where Pres. Obama ate occasionally. We toured a Civil War Museum and stopped at other scenic sites. Believe it or not, Ms. Virgie was the only driver there and back from NYC to Memphis. Mama and I drove from Memphis to Jackson.

Soon Big Will visited us. His friend Trucker lived in Las Vegas, but he also had a residence or family in Virginia. Everyone called him Trucker because he was an over-the-road truck driver. On several occasions he dropped Big Will off at our house and drove to Virginia. He was like Ms. Virgie; he could drive for long stretches at a time. He drove Big Will from Las Vegas to Mississippi and from Mississippi to Las Vegas.

Whenever Big Will came to Mississippi he always stayed with us. Between 1999 to 2011, Big Will visited us for three to four weeks at a time. On those visits, Will and Big Will would leave home early and return late. They would make their rounds across the city visiting family and friends. They visited Michelle, Big Will's oldest daughter and her children and grandchildren. Then they would go to Shady Oaks and visit Aunt Rose on Newport St., head to Idaho St. to visit Karen and Brenda Faye. Sometimes he visited his first wife Betty, and Charlotte, the mother of his children, and his brothers, sisters, and other relatives and friends. Before he returned home, Will would hold a fish fry or a barbeque at our house. McGees would be in the building.

Will use to hold long telephone conversations with Odessa and Little Sister when they were alive. He talked to Big Will for hours too. Will loved to talk about the past, his grandparents and his childhood, especially, connected to his memories. When Odessa and Little Sister passed Will complained he didn't have anyone to talk to. When we lost

Odessa and Little, Will leaned more on his Aunt Dorothy. In many ways, Will's aunts and uncles were more like his siblings and his father was more like a brother.

On September 13, 2013, I had two book events in the Mississippi Delta on the same day. After Traa totaled Will's F-150 in 2011, Will and I went to CarMax, and I used my credit to purchase Will a white F-150. The truck was well kept and had been utilized by employees authorized to drive vehicles in the company's fleet. It was nice. Will loved it. Will put the box of books on the back of the truck, zipped down the black bed covering, and drove us to the Robinson-Carpenter Memorial Library in Cleveland, Mississippi for a Luncheon with Books event hosted by the Friends of the Library. This was my first official book event as the author of a commercially published book classified as a textbook. The event was publicized in the *Bolivar Commercial* newspaper.

The audience was mixed with white and black citizens. One lady told us she had attended school with Uncle J-Boy. She remembered the insurrection on September 30, 1962, on the campus of Ole Miss. The news reporter was a young journalist, Courtney Stevens; she was a graduate of Delta State University. During my discussion with the audience, she told us she had never heard of James Meredith when she was assigned to cover the story for my event. She told us the newspaper editor told her to google him and read something about him. The hour went by fast. I sold a few copies of *Odyssey* and my mother's book *My Brother J-Boy*. But *James Meredith: Warrior and the America that created him* was the hot item. It sold for $48.00 each. Several people purchased two books. It was a good day to be an author.

As we packed up the books in the truck, Ms. Shirley, one of

the audience participants walked outside with us. She informed us that my book event integrated the Friends of the Library event. She told me she wanted to help me reach more readers and told me about the Book Gallery, an independently black owned bookstore in Greenville. We exchanged numbers and kept in touch. According to Ms. Shirley prior to my event only white authors were hosted by the Friends Group and when they hosted me local blacks attended the local Lunch with Books event. Will and I learned stories from audiences everywhere we went. I know when it's time to shut up and listen.

Then, we traveled to the library in Charleston. My mother's classmate Melba Taylor and our cousin's cousin James and his wife Mary Micou attended my event. I met others whose family members ordered books through the mail. Melba Taylor told me they use to call my daddy and mama "Fatty and Skinny." She recalled that my mother met my father at Mississippi Valley when Jackson State College played Valley in Itta Bena. I had never heard that story before. That was a personal story. According to her my parents started dating in the 1958-1959 school year.

A news article was printed in the *Bolivar Commercial* newspaper, Sunday, September 15, 2013. The president of the Friends Group Ms. Sheriton mailed me a clip of the article featuring a large photograph of me autographing books in the library. I framed the picture and hung it in our kitchen. The Friends group paid me an honorarium and my books sales from both events added up nicely. We were looking up baby.

In October of 2013, Will, mama, and I traveled to Caraway Conference Center in Sophia, North Carolina. We stopped in Columbia, South Carolina and stayed at mama's childhood friend Ms. Julia Ann Foster Walker's house. She gave us a tour of her collection of paintings. Some of Ms. Julia Ann's art was on canvas. She told us she had exhibited her art at libraries in Kosciusko and in South Carolina. She told Will and I her grandmother was a talented artist too; her grandmother had to allow white women to claim her art as their own to sell it in Kosciusko during the Jim Crow south. She also told us when she was young, she loved story books and one of the white librarians in Kosciusko would hold up a book in the window of the library and let her read one page at a time through the window in the evenings until she finished the book.

Ms. Julia was a great storyteller. I visualized her standing outside the library looking up at the window reading the picture book. I felt sorry for the girl Julia standing outside a window reading. The story stayed in my memory. Plus, her grandmother was not good enough to sell her own art to the public.

Will and I drove to Applebee's near Ms. Julia Ann's house that night. As we enjoyed hot wings and cocktails, we discussed her storytelling, and we talked about the wide range of art in her collection. We enjoyed each other's company. We often sat on the same seat as newlyweds. Other times we sat across from each other and looked each other in the eyes over a meal and conversation. Sometimes we held hands. Sometimes we found each other in our parts of our house or on the grounds of a site or in the lobby or in a sitting area.

Lionel Richie put it this way, "Just to be close to you girl." ... for the moment baby... yah! yah!

Once we arrived at the Conference Center, Starry asked

Will to pick up several people from the nearby airport. Will was in better health and driving again. He had just learned how to use GPS on his cell phone; they got lost. Anyway, they finally made it to the center. During one field trip, we toured an old school which closed in the 1970s after schools integrated. It was interesting because a community group converted the old school into a senior citizen living center which we thought was genius.

October 31, 2013 was a special day for me as an author. I was the author of a new book *James Meredith: Warrior and the America that created him* which was classified a textbook and landing in college libraries across the globe. Will and I looked out the window as the charter bus we and others occupied rode up the highway from the conference center to Greensboro, North Caroline where I was scheduled to do a joint book event with Shirley Sherrod. I was very appreciative of the opportunity to be on stage with Shirley to discuss and autograph my books.

Will was so proud. He invested in my career. We had purchased a box of books to the tune of $28.80 per book which was my author discount through my publisher Praeger Publisher - 40 percent off the retail price of $48.00. We toured the International Civil Rights Center Museum in Greensboro, North Carolina. One of the original four black college students who sat at the Woolworth Lunch Counter in that very building in 1960 was at our event. He took a group picture with us afterward. Staff from a nearby university were in attendance.

I could hear Will coughing while he was taking my video. He was still plagued with a fungus on his lungs. As always, he was front and center documenting my journey. At times Will struggled to hold the video. He had joint and chronic pain. But he captured my presentation because it was important to him.

I had two books to sell that day. My former classmate Nancy from Montana introduced me. I spoke. Then, Shirley was introduced; she spoke. Shirley and I signed and sold books that evening which was a big deal to me because no other famous author has ever allowed me to sit beside him or her to sale books since that day. As such, RDLN and Shirley Sherrod are valuable social capital. My book later landed in the college library at the University of North Carolina at Greensboro, the University of North Carolina at Chapel Hill, Duke University, North Carolina State University, and Chowan University, also in North Carolina.

Shirley Sherrod and Meredith Coleman McGee autographing and signing books. Twila Martin-Kekahbah standing. Will and a guest near the Exit sign.

The museum staff presented Shirley and me with a gold

box containing a gold Christmas ornament displaying the International Civil Rights Center Museum logo. Will and I decorated our Christmas tree with that ornament from the Christmas of 2013 to 2020 which was our last Christmas together. For Thanksgiving in 2013 we hosted family for dinner. Normally, my younger sister Willa and her children came by. Sometimes Will's nephew Buck or my cousin Jessica and her children came by.

Will always made his rounds to visit his large family on Holidays. He would stop to see his sister next to him, Michelle. Then he headed to Shady Oaks to visit Aunt Rose, Brenda Faye, Karen. He visited Aunt Dorothy in North Jackson. Will had the same routine on Christmas. Will seldom left home on New Year's Eve. We brought in every New Year together.

The following year on December 20, 2014, I presented a *Hand Sale Award* to Will in our den. We were a team. He was selling my books as much as he could. My cousin Ty Patterson was presented the *Best Sales Award* for *Southern Jewel: The Element Within*. Starkishia was presented *Best Literature* for her memoir *Starkishia: Estrella*. William Trest was presented *Most Library Sales* for *Reverse Guilty Plea*. He spent months calling librarians and getting his book on library shelves.

Will surprised me and had Traa make an award for me which was titled *Most Valuable Player*. Traa had been the *Most Valuable Player* on his high school basketball team at Saint Andrews in 2010-2011. At that time, Meredith Etc had four authors. Around 20 people attended our Award Program in our den. The authors sold books to people in the audience. Everyone enjoyed the program and the food and refreshments.

The Christmas of 2015 was one of the most memorable holidays I had with Will. He reached a serious milestone that Christmas. By then, our circle was smaller, and I went visiting with Will. Usually, I was at home, and Will visited his family by himself or with his brother Poncho or cousins or friends. By now we were becoming clingy porch potatoes. I watched basketball playoffs with Will. We watched the Super Bowl at home. In the past, we went to Karen's house four or five years in a row to watch the Super Bowl. Most of us are Saints fans.

Back to the story, I drove Will to his sister's house in West Jackson. We walked in and spoke to Michelle, her husband Kevin, and everyone there. There are usually many family members at Michelle's house. Her husband Kevin is a barber; he cuts the hair of many men in the family and neighborhood. Michelle mentioned their biological mother, Melvin, to Will. Michelle had a relationship with their mother, but Will did not.

Will had a relationship with their brother, Andrew, Melvin's second son, and sister Jackie, Melvin's youngest child and her younger brother Michael. Will and I met Michael around 2000.

He drove up in front of our house and said, "Hey I'm looking for William Earl McGee Jr." Will and I snapped our heads looking at each other.

Then Will responded, "This is him." We focused on him walking across our grass toward Will seated in a chair on our porch.

When Michael reached the porch, he said, "Hey I'm your

Uncle Michael. My niece Jackie told me you lived here. She told me I would know your house by that yellow Dodge (1979) which he was driving every day then."

They shook hands and opened a channel of communication from that moment on. Michael stopped by occasionally and they developed a personal relationship. One day Uncle Mike presented Will with a letter or a series of letters from Melvin.

Will told me the contents of the tablet were personal; he asked me not to read it and I did not. One thing I learned in my half a century of existence was everything about my husband is not my business and everything about me ain't his business. Will once overheard me tell my grandmother something I had never revealed to him. He was crushed. I told her and not him. Now, the shoe was on the other foot, and I understood his need for privacy. I got it. I never looked. I never will. I don't want to know everything. I learned things in my lifetime I wish I hadn't. Life is complicated. Everyone doesn't need to know everyone's complications.

Anyway, I drove us up Robinson Road to Melvin's apartment. Michelle, Will, and I walked in her apartment. Jackie and her husband Keith and one of Melvin's male neighbors (he was a best friend) were sitting in her living room. She spoke to Michelle and when she saw Will she just jumped. Her neighbor stood. Then Melvin yelled waiving her hand toward her neighbor, "Sit down! That's my first born." She walked directly in front of Will and grabbed him by his face and pulled his face almost kissing close to her face. Then she pushed his face back and pulled it close again.

There were so many emotions moving in that room. All eyes were on Melvin and her first born. For those few minutes Will submitted to the woman who carried him in her womb and brought him into the world, the woman who named him for his father, and the woman who gave Will to his father's mother to raise. For those few minutes Will belonged to Melvin. He belonged to his mother.

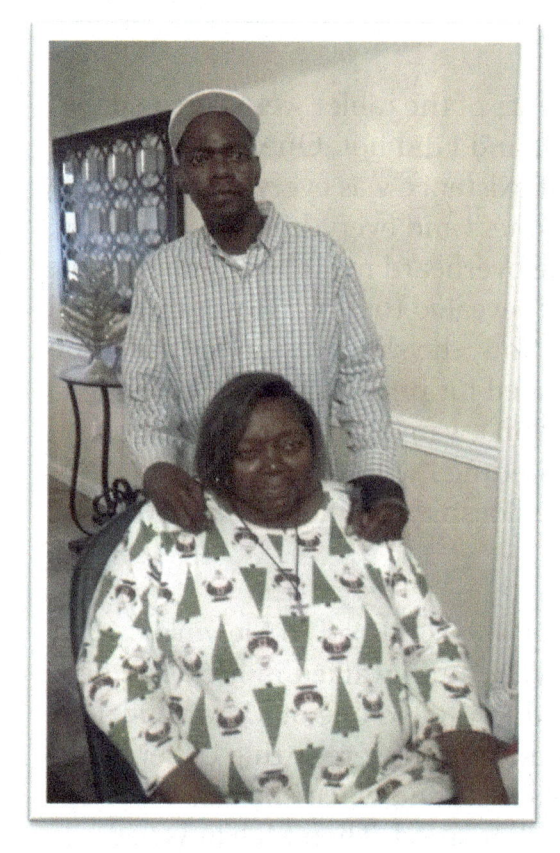

Finally, a mother and her first born were united after 45 years. Mercy! According to Will, Big Will took, Will, age 5, Michelle, age 4, and Karen, a toddler to see Melvin and their grandmother who lived in the Dixon near JSU in 1970. Will told me later he felt nothing but love in those moments his mother was gripping his face in her hands. She hadn't touched me and I felt strong emotions.

I felt the warmth, the longing, the bond, the emptiness, and the reunion. As his wife, I felt so much joy for my husband and my mother-in-law. Healing their broken bond was not magical. It was a slow and gradual process. Nothing significant happened immediately. I recalled enjoying her sweet potato pie on one occasion, and a conversation here and there.

Will, Christmas 2019, his sister Jackie and Keith's house

I eventually met Will's Aunt Sharon, Melvin's younger sister. Will knew Daphne. She had a child with Will's first cousin Fred McGee Jr. Fred's son named, Fred, was double related to Will. Will knew Daphne and his second Cousin Fred from birth. Fred III and Traa were born the same year.

I met Daphne at the Convenience Store next to Napa on Highland Drive in passing when Traa was attending Peeples Middle School. She grabbed Will, hugged him and made a remark, "Boy come here. I'll whoop your butt."

Will introduced me as his wife. He told me she was his aunt and the mother of Little Fred's son. Will told me when he was in his mid-20s, Little Fred was dating Daphne and tried to introduce Will to his mother. Will rejected the introduction. He was bitter and angry. He admitted he was disrespectful. He told me his grandmother asked him to make amends with his mother. She felt Will would need her and need to learn his medical history.

His position was, "She knew where we were. She knew we were at 2504." Big Will told me his first three children were with Melvin. He recalled she was his first love and that she broke his heart. I know little about the different shades of this story. I don't know her side. I know this, Will found peace in his forgiveness of his mother. We spent Christmas of 2019 at Keith and Jackie's house in Byram. To our pleasant surprise, there were Christmas gifts under Jackie's tree for us.

The Christmas of 2019 was magical. Will took pictures with his Aunt Sharon, his Aunt Daphne, his Uncle Mike, and his cousins. He posed standing beside and behind his mother. I knew him well enough to know those were special moments. Finally, time was bringing this estranged mother and son together. They were learning things about each other. She was very inquisitive.

She asked him what kind of fish he liked. She told him what kind of songs she liked. She discussed her mother and her older sister Jackie with Will. She told Will she prayed for him every day. She informed us she prayed to have the opportunity to see all her children again and to meet all her grandchildren and great grandchildren. Redemption is a gift from God.

I'm not sure what Will discussed with his father, or his Aunt Dorothy, or sisters Michelle and Karen about his renewed relationship with his mother. He discussed her with me. Their relationship was getting stronger. I believe Christine McGee was smiling in heaven.

Big Will moved to Vegas in October of 1999. Twenty years later, he was still living in North Vegas near a military base. There was a three-hour difference in time. Big Will had Deloris dial Will's cell phone at 12 midnight our time often at other times nightly. If he called when I was awake, I spoke to him and Deloris. But, many times, he called in the middle of the night. Will and Big Will talked for hours. Will discussed any and everything with his father.

Sometimes Big Will mediated our conflicts over the phone. Big Will use to say, "Somebody got to have some sense. You can't argue by yourself. We can't switch up this late in the game." My father-in-law and I had a personal relationship; he was a great southern father-in-law.

He always did special things. He gave me two bundles of artificial flowers in glass containers when we first moved in our house. He put them in our kitchen where the flowers have remained. Since then, he has given me watches and jewelry. He told many stories about his father and family and even his visits to Canton to Aunt Ora's house. Aunt Ora had a farm in Canton. When Big Will stayed with them during the summers, he and his cousins completed chores. Will told me his grandfather used to get his friends to help them around the house at 2504 and at the hog pen too.

Early in our relationship Will and I attended his Great Aunt Ora's funeral in Canton; we have visited Aunt Ora's daughter Zelma many times since then. Zelma is the only McGee from her generation on the land in Canton. She purchased land for herself across the street from the land her mother and uncles purchased together before her time. Zelma called Will often. Will had great relationships with his father's first cousins. Will use to tell his aunts, "I was raised by the same people who raised you." I guess his point was he was smart.

He was special to so many people. One night when we were dating, Will and I went out and Uncle Butch walked to the living room door and told us, "Ya'll clean tonight. Ya'll have fun." They treated Will like a young prince. He was Big Will and Melvin's first born. They were both 19-years-old when

Will was born. Will was the oldest of 15 or 16. Plus, Will had dozens of siblings by other mothers. He had many mothers: Betty Jean, Ola Mae, Charlotte, Millie, Ruth, Hazel...

During the summer of 2019, Will and I planned our 20th Wedding Anniversary. Spanky helped Will clean the yard. Spanky pressured washed the house too. Will spared no expenses to get things in order. He purchased a new refrigerator, a new sink for our guest bathroom, and eight folding chairs. He had limbs cut down and some woodwork done. Will spilled some white paint on the patio, so Will took the paint brush and drew large jumbo numbers (20th Yr.) on the patio.

When I walked outside, I was pleasantly surprised to see the large white numbers. The 20th Yr. sign on the concrete which didn't even appear to be the result of an accident.

Spanky painted the concrete a red brick color, but they ran out of paint and that project was incomplete on our anniversary. The show went on. I decorated the tables and cooked the food for our special day. Mama cooked salmon croquettes. Our neighbors attended. Most had attended our wedding in 1999.

Our next-door neighbor to our left Henry (unc) was the Master of Ceremony. Nicole and the Quinns were present. Odetta, our next-door neighbor to our right brought a cake which was the only cake on the menu. Someone promised to make a cake but forgot. Mr. Govan and Mrs. Helen Govan were front and center. Uncle J-Boy, Aunt Judy, Uncle Claudel, Aunt Mary, Charlet, Khadiya, Jessica, Will's younger sister Jackie and her husband Keith, and his cousin Spanky were present. Our friends Karon and Carrie, Earnestine, and Ms. B, Pastor Lisa Williams, Tim C. Lee, and others were in attendance. A few people ... Ant and Poncho missed the ceremony and stopped by afterward. The ceremony was less than 15 minutes. I wrote my vows. To my surprise Will did not write his vows. He said his vows from the top of his crown. I felt my vows were too formal since Will did not have any formal vows. Aunt Judy recorded our vow renewal event. Thank you, Aunt Judy.

Will said:

"Twenty years we went down sideways, every way it went. I love you today. I love you tomorrow. I love you with everything. I need you in my corner. I want you in my corner. You are my life. I love you, Meredith."

One line in my vows was, "I love you from the top of my head to the bottom of my feet." Will's expression went from dead serious to laughter because I said to him his famous line.

My vows started with:

"I chose you as my partner for life and now you are my best friend. I promise to stand by you and challenge you. I promise to be great to you...."

I read my love poem *15 Years with Will* to Will which I wrote to him on our 15th wedding anniversary. I also read *The Stranger's Spring*.

We really enjoyed our guests. Mr. Govan, Mrs. Govan, and their daughter were the last of our guests to leave. The Govans celebrated their 70th wedding anniversary on the 20th of June that year.

I remember in 1999 Mr. Govan told Will a story when they counseled us. Mr. Govan said:

> There was once a man who was so in love with his wife. One of his friends passed by the couple's house and saw the man helping his wife hang clothes on a clothesline in their backyard. The friend told the husband, "If she was my wife, I wouldn't help her hang clothes on the clothesline." One day, the ex-husband passed by his ex-wife's house; she had married the man's friend. He was in the back yard helping his wife put clothes on the clothesline.

Perhaps the story has several morals. **One,** be careful who you take advice from. **Two,** what happens between a couple is between them. **Three,** don't allow anyone to talk negatively about your spouse. **Four,** everyone doesn't have decent moral values. **Five,** sometimes, people want what you have. **Six,** if it breaks easily it isn't meant to be.

Will and I were meant to be. We weathered many storms, got up, put one foot in front of the other, and held hands while walking in the rain or under the rainbow.

I think the greatest lesson Will and I learned is that nothing and no one is above the union of a man and a woman. A union is sacred. We supported each other in sickness and in health and in financially good times and in hard times. During our marriage, I was laid off work after the purchase of our home and after the purchase of my 2001 Nissan Maxima. One year Will and I both had surgeries a month apart. Will sought support from human services to get our light bill paid. Will had more health challenges than I did. But we never counted. Tit for tat doesn't work. I was happy and honored to have the strength to be a caregiver to my husband. My Aunt Mary told me before we married not to let anyone talk about my husband.

During the Pandemic, I fainted because I choked when my food went down the wrong way in my windpipe. Will was there when it happened. I was so thankful. I fell on the corner of the dresser hard. He helped me get off the floor.

Then, Will said, "Oh, you hit that dresser hard. Let's get some ice. You gonna' have a black eye tomorrow."

He added, "They gone think I did it." Ha Ha.

Will and I matured over the years. We got to a point where we could feel one another. I knew when he was uncomfortable. He knew when I was uncomfortable. We knew when it was time to go.

Will liked to free-style. I typed the lyrics to *Will's Tape Recording* during the Pandemic. I purchased him a tape recorder so he could recite his thoughts and rhymes on those nights he couldn't sleep. Will had chronic pain. Sometimes pain woke him up.

Will's Tape Recording

What should I do about my dreams? I dream about day and night with a scuffle and fight. Why don't I do it when I'm woke? Sometimes it feels like, it's realized. This is my day-to-day dream. I got to work all day, work all night in my sleep fixing and repairing - doing something. Go with the hustle, bustle, and the flow. But you know what? I'm tired of doing this. I'm happy with my life. I am stepping one step ahead. ... bud snapping, snapping move!

Somebody gone get this here – all this intelligence and knowledge... I hope this is a great day and night.

I don't worry about nothing, not a thang' but my pocket change.

They can throw a granite on me – straight granite - no salt - no water - no shade – just straight granite. But you know what. I'd rather (inaudible) than granite.

I'm still gone make it. Knowledge throwing boulders, throwing boulders!

Don't care 'bout it."

Niggah can't stop me. Nobody can't stop me. Nobody

can't stop me. Nobody can't stop me. Catch you at the front. Back pass you.

Lyrics by William E. McGee Jr. 2020-2021

Will and I went through a lot. Will loved who I loved. I loved who he loved. Christel squeezed my hand while lying in her ICU bed at Central Mississippi Medical Center before she passed. When I met Junior, he was in a nursing home. He stared at me. Will leaned down and Junior said something to Will. Then, Will said, "I think you remind Uncle Junior of Christel when she was young."

When Jermaine broke out of prison, our pain was reopened over the loss of Odessa because Jermaine took her life. Will and I held each other all night. We cried. Will and I talked to Little the morning she died. Will saw Eddie B take his last breath. He called me. I heard the fear in his voice and rushed to the Baptist Hospital to the ER. Will and I sat in the family room for 20-minutes waiting for the family to arrive.

My older brother Bobby's straw hat is on a nail in our bedroom. Will felt pain that his Uncle Ronnie was murdered on his 18th birthday. Ronnie took Will to see Michael Jackson at the Coliseum when Will was five years old. Ronnie took Will to see James Brown too. Will had a personal relationship with my brother Ronnie. Will wanted to go to Chicago to pay respects to my brother when he died on Father's Day in 2019.

Will found a bracelet made of silver elephants and bought it for me as a symbol of the figurines my Grandmother Beulah collected. She collected elephants and she left her collection of elephants to me in her will. Will travelled with me to Georgia to visit my Uncle Everett, to St. Petersburg, Florida to visit my Aunt Miriam, and we travelled to Buffalo every other year. On those visits to Buffalo, Will and I had the upstairs apartment to ourselves.

In 2019, Big Will developed new health issues. Will and I talked back and forth with Moony and Poncho who were in and out of the hospital. Sometimes we spoke with Big Will's girlfriend, Deloris. After Big Will got out of the hospital, and started recovering, I had a tough time understanding him. I asked Will, "Did you understand him?" Will told me half of the time he didn't understand what Big Will said.

I lost my grandmother on June 26, 2017. I visited her in March of 2017; the visit was a gift. I treasured my time with my grandmother three months before her passing. In fact, Trucker had driven Big Will to our house when I went to the Women's Conference in NYC in March of 2017 and to Buffalo to visit my grandmother for a few days. Trucker passed afterward and Will missed a year or so visiting Mississippi. Over a 20-year span, Big Will's yearly visits from Las Vegas dropped from three to four weeks every year to three to four days. I thought it was time to visit Big Will. I planned another trip to Las Vegas.

CHAPTER 3
Pandemic

I ordered two tickets to Las Vegas in February of 2020. There was a cheaper flight from Memphis which connected in Denver. So, I booked that flight and called Ms. Dorothy to see if I could leave my CTS Cadillac at her house for two weeks. She was happy to help. She told me to call if we needed directions to her house.

On March 2, 2020, Will and I travelled to Marion, Alabama to volunteer to work on Billie Jean Young's campaign on Super Tuesday. She was running for Alabama State Board of Education in District 5. Billie Jean made reservations for me and Will at Bennett Suites Bed and Breakfast in Marion. I told Will, "We came to help Billie Jean and she put us in luxury."

A Black couple owned the business. The wife was an avid reader; she stored an amazing collection of books by Black authors on bookshelves throughout the bed and breakfast. I walked through the rooms reading book spines. I had read some books, others I had not read. Will got comfortable on the couch, turned on the television, and got on his cell phone. We watched television for a while, showered, and retired to the master suite. We got cozy in the king size bed on the jumbo mattress.

The next morning, we drove to Billie Jean's house a few blocks away for coffee and to get campaign push cards. To my surprise Alice Thomas-Tisdale, Publisher, Jackson Advocate, newspaper was present at Billie Jean's house drinking coffee too. I was drinking coffee with two of my mentors. Will knew them both. I am a contributing writer for the Jackson Advocate where I started writing professionally in December of 1993.

Billie Jean had driven 100 miles from Judson College with a student to attend my first Barnes & Noble book event in Tuscaloosa, Alabama in 2013. Billie Jean and Alice attended my Barnes & Noble event in Jackson in 2019 when the 2nd edition of *James Meredith: Warrior and the America that created him* was released by Meredith Etc.

Will originally met Billie Jean and Starry in 1999 in Greenwood, Mississippi. We drove to break-bread with Billie Jean and Starry the fall after we married. Will and I had also broken bread with Billie Jean in New Orleans. Will and I use to listen to Billie Jean's poetry on cassette tape.

Over a cup of coffee that morning, Billie Jean asked Will to pass out push cards in Selma, Alabama at the courthouse. Billie Jean told us we would have to work separate post today. I went to the voting precinct down the street from the famous church where activists congregated after the Selma March in 1965. As we were driving to our destinations, Will said, "I never worked on a campaign before." We had been married over 20 years and that was news to me.

We arrived in Selma and used our GPS to find the courthouse and a campaign worker explained to us how to get to the polling location across the street from the projects which contained red bricks; it looked like the Gadsden Street Projects where my Aunt Cat and my cousins grew up. Most poll workers were working for Billie Jean's opponents. They knew each other. I was Billie Jean's only worker at that polling place pushing cards for Billie Jean. One of the male workers decided to call me "Mississippi."

I was talking and asking questions and learned I was two buildings near a famous church which contained famous pictures. One of Coretta Scott King's classmates walked up. Everyone greeted her. She had been voting at that precinct since the 1960s. The journalist section of my brain kicked in and I asked a few questions.

She told me, "I went to school with Coretta. When it rained her father would drive her to school in a buggy." That was enough information for me to know Ms. Coretta's family had a little something in the 1940s. That was the first time I heard of a Black girl being transported to school in a buggy.

I worked hard competing to push Billie Jean's cards to approaching voters in my space. "Vote Billie Jean Young," I said loudly to citizens. I had to compete with at least three people who were yelling, "Vote Tonya Chestnut." When Ms. Chestnut came to bring lunch to her workers, they showed her so much love and one introduced me to her. I had the pleasure of taking a picture with her. Billie Jean called for us to meet them for lunch, but Will was already in line at Churches Chicken. We were at Churches missing an opportunity for better food. I ordered fried okra and corn on the cob. Will ordered chicken breast and fries.

Will told me he was having a great time meeting people at the courthouse, and they had somewhere to sit. He was happy and I was happy he was happy. After I returned to the polling place after lunch, I continued my routine "Vote Billie Jean Young" and passed out push cards and talked to workers. A tour bus full of mostly whites pulled up in front of the church; some tourists walked where we were and asked us questions. Many were from California touring Civil Rights sites in the south.

One of Ms. Chestnut's workers volunteered to take me through the back door of the church to see the pictures of MLK and others lined up on the basement wall. She led me through the back door. I took pictures of historical pictures on the wall. We peeped through the pulpit door and heard someone telling the tourists historical facts about the church and its role in the Civil Rights movement. One of the tourists used her hand and fingers to beck for us to enter. We declined and went back to our precinct posts.

That night the campaign workers gathered at By the River Center for Humanity on Water Ave. The front of the facility faces the Edmund Pettus Bridge where John Lewis and others were beaten and trampled by horses in 1965; the rear is off the

Alabama River. Afriye Wekandodis is the founder and owner of the museum. After dinner she gave us a tour and Will and I looked at the artifacts in the facility. She unlocked the back door and we walked to the river with her. She told us that during slavery times her facility was a holding center and auction block for slaves. She told us that the ships anchored on the riverbed there and slaves walked and entered the building. Groups across the country frequent her center to partake in her performances and dramatizations of slave life.

Will, Alice Tisdale, Billie Jean, Wendall Paris, Billie Jean's nieces and I and other workers watched the campaign results in a sitting area near the rear door. The crowd grew smaller after the 10 pm news. By then, Joe Biden was the presumptive nominee for the Democratic Party. Biden would face off against Pres. Trump in the general election. Tonya Chestnut was in the lead. But we were hopeful because Billie Jean was not far behind. By the next morning, it was clear Chestnut had more votes. Fred Bell won. Billie Jean told me she would never put her hat in the political ring again.

I thought she would have been the perfect person for the job. Will and I were happy we had been a part of her political experience. A year later, March 30, 2021, we lost Billie Jean, a friend to the end. Billie Jean was a native of Nahcola, Alabama located in rural central Alabama in the "Black Belt" region. She was the daughter of sharecroppers. She became a lawyer, a playwright, and an advocate for her race. She was a founding board member of the Rural Development Leadership Network. She encouraged me to write poetry. Will and I called her our friend. She was known nationally for her one-woman show depicting the life of Fannie Lou Hamer.

We left Alabama March 4, 2020, and drove back home. That Saturday, Will brought Jaquan to the Learning Tree Book Club meeting at the Jackson Medical Mall. We had our roundtrip tickets to Las Vegas; we were excited about our trip.

On March 10, 2020, I drove Will to Memphis. That night we went to several dollar stores looking for masks and plastic gloves because we heard there was an airborne disease spreading and airlines were requiring people to wear masks. Unfortunately, everyone was out of masks. We did find a small box of gloves at Walmart. That night we went to the home of Dorothy Mays James to spend the night and leave our car at her house until we returned from Las Vegas March 25, 2020.

The morning of March 11th, Ms. Dorothy got up and fixed breakfast. She cooked pork sausage. I don't eat pork. Will ate and I drunk coffee. Then Ms. Dorothy took us to the dialysis clinic. She told me and Will to go to the facility with her.

We walked in and she said, "This is my family. They are boarding a flight in a few minutes. Can you give them a mask?"

The attendant said, "Yes. Wait one minute." She went away for a minute and returned with two masks.

Ms. Dorothy thanked the attendant. Then she passed the masks to me. Will and I thanked the attendant and Ms. Dorothy. Ms. Dorothy smiled pleasantly and titled her head - a habit of hers.

We got in her car, and she said, "I'm not supposed to be driving." Her physician asked her not to drive when she became a kidney dialysis patient. Then we returned to her car, and she drove up Winchester Rd. to the Memphis International Airport.

I did not hug Ms. Dorothy because news reporters were advising against physical contact. We got our luggage out of the trunk of her car, I headed to the driver's side and told Ms. Dorothy thank you. She smiled and drove off. Will and I walked in the airport with our faces covered with light blue surgical masks, pulling our luggage; then, we found our gate, took a seat beside each other, and waited.

On the 11th, there were no reported cases of COVID 19 in Mississippi. We didn't know what to expect. When we left Mississippi on the 10th there were 270 new COVID cases in the USA. By the time we boarded the plane there were 245 new cases.

The plane was packed. There were people in first class two seats on each side of the isle; there were three seats on each side of the isle in the general seating section. I believe there were 238 seats on the flight. Will and I had cough drops to take because we did not plan to cough and scare anyone. Neither one of us coughed. Will walked to the restroom once. Our connecting flight was in Denver, Colorado.

Will and I walked in the airport in Denver, and we were surprised because through our face covering the air smelled polluted. I took Clorox cleaning wipes and wiped the chairs before Will and I sat down. I was concerned about Will being exposed to germs because of his compromised immune system. I walked to McDonalds while Will sat and watched our luggage. I waited in line but returned to our seat without purchasing any beverages. We had water during the previous flight.

Will said, "It smells polluted here." Our boarding station was near a room where people were allowed to smoke cigarettes which contributed to the strong odor we smelled.

I told Will, "Yes, I have never seen an airport this unsanitary in my life." We were relieved to board the plane and get away from Denver. When we arrived at the airport in Las Vegas it was so clean. The pictures of Frank Sinatra and Redd Foxx were sparking clean. The windows were clean. The air smelled clean. Will and I had talked to Ola Mae at least four times before we arrived. She wanted to know when we were arriving. Ola Mae was checking in with Moony about picking us up.

We pulled our luggage and snapped pictures as we walked through the airport. I thought about all those road trips we took over the years and how constantly we listened to cassette tapes of Redd Foxx and Richard Pryor. We listened to "Live and Dirty Volume 3 For Adults Only by Redd Foxx so many times. He had a joke where a woman walked in on him with a woman and he said, "Don't believe your lying eyes." It was so funny every time.

The Preacher's Wife Original Soundtrack I loved so much. Will and I both enjoyed "My Name is Black" a collection of spoken word poems by Billie Jean Young. Eventually, I replaced cassette tapes and albums with CDs. On road trips we listened to "Song of Solomon" by Toni Morrison read in her voice. Traa and my nieces and nephew Joss enjoyed *Song of Solomon* too.

We stood in the Arrival section at the Las Vegas airport for 30 minutes or so because it took Moony a minute to find our gate. When she arrived, we were happy to see her. She was happy to see us. We loaded our luggage in the trunk of her car; she told us, "Mama wants me to bring ya'll over later. She has something planned at Uncle Dons." Moony drove us to North Las Vegas to Big Will and Deloris's apartment.

We got out and Big Will came to the door. He seemed surprised to see us. We went in and hugged him and Deloris. We put our luggage in the extra bedroom. Big Will offered us everything in sight: something to drink, coffee, cookies, and food. We were so happy to be there. Deloris and I conversed. Will conversed with his dad. Big Will and Will went outside and sat in chairs on the front patio. Neighbors stopped by and Big Will introduced people to Will.

A few people already knew or knew of Will. Will and I walked to the store for ice and something to drink several times. Their apartment was next to a strip mall with five or six businesses including a BBQ establishment ran by the grandmother of Moony's grandchildren. The grandmother and Deloris were friends. There was a taco establishment, a laundromat, and a convenience store. The clerk at the Taco establishment gave us free ice every day.

As we were walking to the store, a young guy drove by and yelled out the window, "What's up Lil Will." Will waved his hand at the guy whose car was rolling by slowly as he spoke.

I asked Will, "Who was that? Who knows you here?"

Will replied, "He is from the neighborhood (meaning Shady Oaks). Poncho probably told him I was coming." I know most people Will know like George Berry, but I didn't know the person driving that car.

That evening Moony called me on my cellphone and said, "Hey sis, I'm pulling up."

Deloris asked, "Was that Moony?

"Yah'" I replied.

'Ya'll go on and walk out there. Have fun, Deloris added." Big Will walked up the sidewalk with us and stood outside until Mooney pulled up. After she pulled up, she said, "Hey daddy." He spoke. We spoke. I hopped on the front seat. Will got on the back seat. Moony drove off to her uncle's apartment in North Vegas within driving distance of a Mountain view. We walked up the stairs to the apartment; we were greeted by family members: Ed, Ola Mae, Don, Monica, Adrene, Neecie, Brandon, Deasia, and Akasia.

It was so nice to see everyone. Will and I hadn't seen Brandon and his mother since he was five years old. We hadn't seen Adrene since he and the kids spent a few days with us, and the boys mowed our lawn. Will knew Don and his wife. It was my first time meeting them. Mooney comes to Mississippi every other year. Jeffery bought Mooney, Avion, Deasia and Akasia by our house to see us in 2018. Will and Poncho went to Pelahatchie often to see Ed and Ola Mae. We talked, took pictures, and the younger crowd followed each other to Moony's spot for food, drinks, pool, and gaming. Will and Brandon played pool. We chit chatted, asked questions, and caught up. We enjoyed each other's company.

Brandon followed Mooney when she drove us back to Big Will's apartment. He got out of the car and conversed with his grandfather for a minute. On our third day in Vegas, Moony picked us up; then, she picked up Ola Mae and drove us to the strip to buy souvenirs. We planned to catch a movie during our visit, but within five days of our visit, March 17, 2020, Mayor Carolyn G. Goodman's ordinance shut down the strip (tourist sites, casinos...).

Every morning at 7 am Will and I watched the local news. Pres. Trump, Anthony Fauci and the national medical team discussed COVID 19. Will and I were glued to the television every morning. The news report about this Pandemic, an air borne disease, and the massive loss of life was frightening. Deloris, her neighbor, and I stood in food lines sponsored by Feeding America at a nearby school. They distributed fresh fruit, water, canned goods, snacks, and fresh meat. Deloris's friend drove us to the grocery store one day and we noticed that various shelves were bare.

One morning Will and I heard there was a reported case of the coronavirus at the military base near Big Will's apartment. That was alarming news. Will and I were obeying the scientist, socially distancing, washing our hands, and wearing our masks. By the 15th, Big Will and his friend Ms. Tina had a double house birthday party. Big Will put on his red suit, his hat, and his shoes. He was ready. Deloris got dressed too.

Normally, she stays in the house.

Some people sat outside, and some people sat inside. We played music and danced in our seats and sang. Ms. Tina knew all the lyrics of one Cardi B song. I was amazed. She was too cool. Deloris got cranked up too. She sang every lyric of "Whatta Man" by Salt and Pepper. "What a man, what a man, what a mighty good man." We had a good old fashioned house party without a soul train line. When Deloris was singing Big Will looked around. He was amazed too.

Man! They got into the story telling. One friend described how she and Big Will became friends and things they use to do. Ms. Tina had her stories. I took pictures and videos and connected to people who lived in the apartment community on Facebook.

The next morning, I saw Ms. Tina. She said to me with a little bass in her voice, "I know you didn't put me on Facebook!" Then, she added, "Mississippi can't handle all this," stretching her arms outward. Then, Ms. Tina burst out laughing. I was relieved. I thought I was in trouble. Big Will laughed. I laughed too. Fun times. Laughing is good for the soul. Big Will had loyal friends. They traded with each other and looked out for each other. Can't beat that!

Everyone in the apartment complex called Big Will, "Pops." Some evenings there were six or more men standing in front of the apartment laughing, drinking, and cracking jokes. Will was sitting outside hanging with them. When he got tired, he retired. I often sat on the bar stool, talked to Deloris, or watched television.

Will and I spent a few days at Moony's apartment she shared with Frank. They lived upstairs. We took our shoes off and placed our shoes in a small section near the front door. I wondered if the flight of stairs was challenging to Will. If climbing the stairs was challenging, he never showed it. He was enjoying his moments with his younger sister. He sat in the kitchen with her. Then, he sat beside me on the couch. Frank shared information with us about mass graves and information he learned about the Pandemic. Moony kept their place clean and neat. A couple of times Will and I walked to the convenience store and the park across the street. We sat on the bench and took pictures.

Moony drove us to the grocery store and to Home Depot where we looked for Clorox wipes and Clorox. The sight of empty shelves in the grocery store, at drug stores, and other retail outlets was frightening. The entire world changed. Fear of the unknown caused people to panic. In the meat market there were barely any packages of meat. Entire sections in the meat department were bare.

After several days, Moony drove us back to Big Will's apartment. Will and I saw news reports about airport closings, flights cancelling, and we started fearing being stuck in Vegas. We didn't know what to expect. We continued our routine. I went wherever Deloris, and her neighbor went. If they stood in a food line, I stood in a food line. That sweet bag of popcorn was good. I walked to the strip mall with Will every day too. One day we had to wash our clothes, and the attendant wouldn't let us in. Deloris walked around there and told them Will was Big Will's son and I was his daughter-in-law. They let us in. After a week, people were speaking to me and Will when they saw us. It was like we had moved into the neighborhood.

Around the 25th of March, Will and I were pulling our luggage from Big Will and Deloris's apartment to the street where Moony was waiting with two of her granddaughters.

A man upstairs yelled, "Ya'll leaving?"

We replied, "Yes."

He said, "I thought ya'll got stuck and couldn't get back home."

Will said, "Naw, we'll didn't' get stuck. We are headed home."

We put the luggage in Moony's car; she drove us to the airport five hours early. There is no place like home. Will and I enjoyed our family; we were ready to get back to our house, our big bed, and our routine. As we checked in our luggage at the counter, we saw a handful of people. We walked through the airport, and we noticed all the restaurants and retail shops were closed. Delta, United, and other airlines had cancelled all flights. We walked a bit to get to our gate. When we found our gate, there were three or four people in the entire section. After we waited three hours, a few more people showed up. Will and I boarded the plane 40 minutes early. Before the flight took off, I thought there were 30 people on the flight which had the capacity to hold at least 238 people. Will thought there were 15 or so people on the plane. Each person on the flight could have had all three seats to themselves. Will and I sat together and looked out the window.

When we were landing in Memphis, we called Ms. Dorothy and she picked us up at the airport. We went inside and she told me she loved *My Picture Dictionary* and *My First Book Series*. I left the books with her to review; she suggested I create a black and white cheaper edition of *My Picture Dictionary* to make the book affordable for more children. I was the main author of both books. The proceeds are donated to Community Library Mississippi, a non-profit which I co-founded and chaired. Ms. Dorothy told me the word 'alphabet' was plural and it needed no 's.'

Ms. Dorothy had over 50 years of experience in early childhood. She was the author of dozens of books for early learners. I was happy to accept instruction from her anytime. I discussed her idea with our board when I returned. Today we sell a hardback ($19.98), softcover full color ($14.98) and a black and white edition ($5.98) of *My Picture Dictionary* by Meredith Coleman McGee at al.

Not long after we crossed the state line into Mississippi, Will and I got on an exit and went to a dollar store to buy tissue and Clorox to take home. The clerk told us there was plenty tissue and Clorox in stock now. Okay, things were getting back to normal. I was relieved to be driving up I-55 South from Memphis headed home. There's no place like home.

When we arrived home and walked in, Khadiya was sweeping the kitchen. There were two boxes of toys which belonged to our great-nephew Amir, a toddler. Will kept a dump truck in the den for Amir. Khadiya and Amir's father use to come to our house to play cards when they were dating. Amir's baby shower was held at our home too. The event was an exceptionally good event because Aunt Miriam, who was born in 1926, attended. Will and I drove, mama, Traa and Khadiya to visit Aunt Miriam in St. Petersburg, Florida when they were in middle school.

Like everyone else, Will and I were stuck in the house. In the mornings he watched Wagon Train, Father Knows Best, Rifle Man, and Leave it to Beaver. When I wasn't typing, which was all the work I had coming in, I watched television with Will. One of my customers brought his forms to the door and I typed it and took it to the curb. Sometimes Will and I sat in the living room and talked. We watched the 10 o'clock news and nightline together every night. Saturday nights we watched *Saturday Night Live*. Sunday mornings we watched *Meet the Press, This Week with George Stephanopoulos*, and *Soledad O'Brien*. Sometimes we listened to the Houston based Preacher Joel Osteen.

During the Pandemic, we watched Netflix series like Selena the Series and movies through Hulu and Amazon Prime: *High Note, Coming 2 America, The United States vs. Billie Holiday*. We were losing so many loved ones and friends. Too many losses. Our love grew stronger and stronger. Will had no insecurities about our love as he did during the early years. At some point I can't pinpoint a day or hour or year, but we stopped arguing and started cherishing life, love, opportunity, food, entertainment, family, loyalty, peace, and fun. We felt blessed to make it home from Vegas. We felt blessed to avoid contacting anyone with the coronavirus. We felt blessed to purchase necessities. We felt blessed to love someone who loves you back.

There are two expressions: *Love the one you with* and *Love who loves you*. Same difference. You can allow someone to suck the blood out of you or you can give to a giver. One concept is different from the other.

One day Will asked me, "Why you love me so much?"

I replied, "I love you because you love me."

He asked me questionable, "That's why you love me?"

Since he didn't like my answer I explained, "I love you because you are a good husband, you always have my back, you care about my goals, you're handsome, you're kind, and you belong to me." He did. He belonged to me. I belonged to him. I saw Will slowing down. He was shorter in statute. His doctor explained Will had lost several millimeters in height because his bone structure was degenerating. Will had chronic pain but he never allowed his disabilities to take over his spirit. Despite suffering with arthritis and pain, every day Will got up and put one foot in front of the other and walked through the door to find a way to be productive. There was not a lazy bone in his body.

Whether it was a project at home or with the car or at someone else's home, Will was on it and ready to get with it. He was slowing down. But he was happy all the time. If he was in pain or his ankles were swollen, I placed pillows under his legs and put the heating pad on the pillow to help ease his pain. He would call me, "Meredith" to get him ice or to fix his plate or to be his legs sometimes. This process became a normal ritual.

Some mornings before Will opened the living room door to leave the house, he looked back at me and said, "Wish me luck." I would wish him well. Then, he told me where he was going. Then, he would say, "I'll be back."

One day in September of 2020, Deloris called and said Big Will was extremely sick. We asked her questions. Aunt Dorothy called. Will called. Moony went by. We felt Big Will should go to the hospital. Ed caught COVID while visiting Vegas and he died. People were afraid to go to the hospital. Eventually, Big Will was hospitalized. At first, he talked to us some when we called. As the weeks went by his health declined.

Big Will had a long 30-day run in the hospital. He spent one night in Hospice and spent his last day on earth at his apartment. I was told his eyes were bright when the ambulance drivers pushed him through the doors of his apartment. I imagined he felt peace to see the pictures of himself in every corner of his living room, the dogs, the bar, the kitchen table, and the hall leading to his bedroom.

Big Will passed away, Sunday, October 11, 2020. It was a sad day for the family. Will said, "When Big Will stopped talking I knew he wasn't going to make it." Facebook lit up that day with pictures of Big Will. There were two children left: Dorothy and Butch. Big Will's body was transferred from the possession of Moony to Will via a conversation with the funeral home in Las Vegas. I called Willis & Sons to find someone to handle the freight containing Big Will. Mrs. Willis returned my call. Mrs. Willis made arrangements to handle Big Will's body. COVID caused shipping delays since there could only be a few boxes of freight containing human remains on each flight. The freight with his remains landed in the Medgar Evers International Airport around October 22nd.

It took over 14 days to get Big Will's freight from Las Vegas to Jackson, Mississippi. I had to go in the funeral home alone to view Big Will's body. Will stayed in the car. I went to view him when they dressed him too. That was my first time viewing a corpse. I prepared Big Will's program for his graveside service which was held October 31, 2020. Big Will was laid to rest at Autumn Wood Cemetery on Northside Drive. Odessa, Little, Eddie B were laid to rest there too. Fred's widow officiated over Big Will's service. Vickie read the obituary and the tributes, and the acknowledgements.

TRIBUTE POEM FROM CHILDREN
Big Will, Big Will by Meredith Coleman McGee

Big Will was our daddy.
Big Will was our friend to the end.
His memories are sealed in our minds.
as long as we stand in this land.
He had nothing but love for his family.
He had nothing but love for his friends.

We miss you daddy.
We love you daddy.
Rest in Power!
Rest in Peace!

We are holding it down.
United your children stand.
Take our hands dear Lord.
Lead us onward.

Love reigns like a flower
to the ninth power!
Love reigns to the root.

From you our branch grows.
Heaven help us all!
Peace be still.
William (Jr.), Michelle, Debra, Karen, Kenneth Earl, Mischa, Umekia, Rashad, Kelsey Dior, Cleo, et al...

Ola Mae, Mooney, Will, Las Vegas 03.13.2020
Will and Meredith on movie night

Will took this picture of Meredith in 2012 in their front yard.
Photos William & Meredith McGee Family Collection

Big Will's death changed Will's perspective about life in general. Will lived every day differently after his father passed. Will was focused. He was playful as always but a little on the serious side too. We grew closer and closer because the Pandemic forced us to spend more time together. We developed new rituals watching television, sitcoms, movies, the news, and talk shows. We watched *The Upshaws, Dad Stop Embarrassing Me, Harlem* and documentaries on Malcolm X, the Watts riot, Nina Simone, Aretha Franklin...

In the winter of 2020, one day, our friend Brenda came by, and I mentioned paying her for a personal loan we owed her for Big Will's funeral.

Will asked, "How much?"

I replied, "$250.00."

Will said, "Okay. I got it. He handed her the cash wiping our slate clean. We had wiped all the slates clean and were moving forward.

Brenda said, "McGee (she called Meredith 'McGee') you acted like you were surprised Will had the money."

I admitted, "I was."

It's interesting as close as Will and I were, we had a level of privacy. Will was raised by his grandparents. I was influenced by my grandparents and my step grandfather Pleasant Thomas. Grandma Roxie told me, "You can't let the right hand know everything the left hand has." If push came to shove, the left hand or the right hand would come up with money. Believe that! If Will needed something I had his back and he definitely had mine. I was paying debt down and Will was stacking. Our goal was to be debt free. By the Spring of 2021, Will was busy as a bee. Spanky and Short drove him to different work sites, etc. Will's wrist and joint arthritis had worsened. Will was getting tight fisted too. I saw some dining room chairs I wanted in April of 2021. Will said, "We can't drive them chairs." I guess the salesman assumed Will was in charge because he walked back to the counter after Will made his statement. Ha Ha.

I reminded Will that Shirley, our family friend from Pensacola was coming to spend a few days with us to write and edit her book of poetry and short stories.

I told Will, "We can't let Shirley sleep on that mattress."

Meredith, Ola Mae, and Will in the kitchen
Photos William & Meredith McGee Family Collection

Will said, "Naw' that mattress almost killed us." Will and I slept in the guest room when we painted the floor in our room because the fumes were so strong. Will and I were buying a new mattress for our guest room because we wanted Shirley to be as comfortable at our house as we were when we spent the night at her house in Pensacola. Spanky helped the salesman put the mattress on the back of Jeffrey's truck; we left those beautiful chairs on the floor display.

McGee Family Reunion-Grove Park-Dorothy McGee, right

Left: Meredith & Will posing in front of Sir Captain's Zimma

Right: Baby James, Jameria, and Will

Traa and Meredith Ty A Patterson's book release party in 2014

New Year's Eve front yard 2015

Kevin, Michelle, and Curtis on Michelle's Birthday

Buck, Calla, Will front. Rear: Khadiya & Eric rear

Left picture Will received Best Hand Sale Award 2014.
Right picture rear Michelle and Will, Angel (black sweater)
Meredith, center, Madison, front center, and Bird, front right.
Will told Bird, "You read this book."

Linda Shoulders repast gathering Dec. 2017

Photos William and Meredith McGee Family Collection

Will posing with Jackson's Mayor Chokwe Antar Lumumba

Will and Meredith with sons of the late Paul Haynes on Newport St., Sam, far right

Family picture Christmas of 2019. Will (white baseball cap),
Melvin seated (Christmas tree sweater)

Left photo: 09.25 2019 - 20th Wedding Anniversary
Right photo: 09.25 2020 - 21st Wedding Anniversary wearing
the white watch Big Will gave Meredith.

William Earl McGee Jr.

Henry (Unc) & Meredith

Meredith & Starry Krueger

Kelsey, Will, & Meredith

Irma Walker & Will

129

Meredith & Will on movie night

The Storyteller (center) who founded Mississippi's first Civil Right Museum in Belzoni, MS. Will and Meredith were guest of Tim C. Lee at Respect Our Black Dollars Banguet.
Rev. George Lee & Fannie Lou Hamer Civil Rights Museum
Helen Sims, 17150 US Hwy. 49, Belzoni, MS 39038
662.936.7761 – helensims@live.com

Will, Judson College, campus, Marion, AL - July 2019

Billie Jean Young and Meredith Tuscaloosa, AL 2013

Marilyn, Brenda ... George Clinton Concert, Jackson, MS

Photo William and Meredith McGee Family Collection
6th dating anniversary Feb. 8, 2004

Photo William and Meredith McGee Family Collection

Michelle Cole-Barnes, green blouse, Will, right 2017

Oct 31, 2020, Repast of Big Will.

Meredith Family Reunion, Daytona Beach, FL Flea Market

Mily, Leticia, Meredith and Will New Mexico, Oct 2017.
Courtesy of William and Meredith McGee Family Collection

Saint Patrick's Day, South Jackson, 2019

Image courtesy William & Meredith McGee Family Collection
Traa wrote notes to Will over the years.

Douglassville, GA at Russell & Karen's apartment - Jennifer and husband, Karen, Will, Meredith, and India, Brandon (boy center) Photo William & Meredith McGee Family Collection

Traa in driveway in 2009 – next photo- the 2 and the 3

William Earl McGee Jr & William Earl McGee III, 2014

Traa holding his Basketball Saint Award 2009-2010

Will headed to a funeral wearing Charlie Hall's suit jacket. Charlie Hall was mother's stepfather; he passed in 1997.

Learning Tree Book Club meeting 03.08.2020
Jackson Medical Mall, 2:30 to 3pm - Will reading the board
behind Jaquan McGee, Morgan, and Vickie

Left photo Will reading the store display sign "Meredith Coleman McGee" at Barnes & Noble, Ridgeland, MS
Right photo near the mural and waterfront in Vicksburg, MS one of Will & Meredith's favorite tourist sites

Billie Jean Young's 70 Birthday Celebration
Judson College, Marion, AL

Will in our driveway in front of our Wisteria tree May 23, 2021

CHAPTER 4
May 30

Sunday, May 30, 2021, Will and I attended the Tulsa George Floyd Memorial Celebration at Battlefield Park which is 3.5 miles from our house off Highway 80. Soon after we arrived, I asked if the restrooms were working. The bathrooms were out of order. So, I drove back to our house so we could use the restroom. Coach Obasi and his wife K'leita invited us to the event. Will and I had also been their guest in March of 2019 at the Respect Our Black Dollars Award Banquet.

The VERDICT 04.20.2021—GUILTY, GUILTY, GUILTY

George Perry Floyd Jr. black male killed during an arrest after a store clerk alleged he passed a counterfeit $20 bill. Derek Chauvin, 1 of 4 police officers on the scene, pressed his knee on Floyd's neck for 9 minutes 29 seconds prompting global protest.

<u>Born</u>: October 14, 1973, <u>Fayetteville, NC</u> (46 years old)
<u>Died</u>: May 25, 2020, <u>Minneapolis, MN</u>
<u>Buried</u>: June 9, 2020, <u>Houston Memorial Gardens, Pearland, TX</u>
<u>Children</u>: <u>Gianna Floyd</u>
Rapper three songs—Sunny Day, 2019

JURY OF FLOYD'S PEERS determined his life matters; set legal precedent of the century by finding former white policemen Derek Chauvin guilty in death of George Floyd...
Blacks (our part) property value uplifts—removing plight, stop littering, stop dumping
Next steps: new investment in black communities—increasing the black business class

---

Will was moving slower that day, but I wasn't alarmed. Will's eyes were snow white. I noticed it. He looked good. We stood for a minute looking for chairs. Coach Obasi noticed and offered us his seats. We sat down. The event was exciting. The various speakers informed us, entertained us, and engaged us. Will and I enjoyed the female African dancers. Then there were a series of speakers. Several elders in the Local Organizing Committee spoke and they advised the audience not to take the vaccine.

Will said, "I'm glad we took it.

I replied, "Me too."

One speaker acknowledged a list of the nationally known victims of police and racial violence such as Duante Wright, George Floyd, Michael Brown, Emmitt Till, Freddie Gray, Breonna Taylor, Tamir Rice, Sandra Bland, Eric Garner, and others. The youth talent expressions, spoken word, and lyrical contests were especially entertaining.

Statistics revealed that black males are 14 times more likely to die from firearms than white males and black women are four times more likely to die from firearms than white females. Today, black genocide whether the result of black on black or blue on black is a public health crisis.

Two of the youth poets Mikaela and Chelsea had participated and won 2nd place prizes in the Jackson Book Festival's poetry contest February 13, 2021, a program under the umbrella of Community Library Mississippi. Will and I thought all the youth were exceptionally talented and incredibly positive. The poems highlighted stories about Black Wall Street. It was inspiring. It was a breath of fresh air to see positivity in a city where gun violence has reached historic highs, and in a Pandemic which was taking people out daily.

After the performance, we greeted people sitting near us. I took pictures with LaRonda Coleman, Mary Coleman's niece. LaRonda performed her song, *Jacktown Love*. Ms. Mary is an 88-year-old author, and gospel group leader and singer. LaRonda started singing in the church. LaRonda converted the lyrics of *Jacktown Love* into a poem, submitted it in the contest and won 1st place in the adult competition at the

Jackson Book Festival. Ms. Mary is a founding member of Community Library Mississippi. Meredith Etc published her memoir "Mary's Story & Song."

Talk it, Walk it, Own it
By Meredith Coleman McGee
January 20, 2021

Talk it, Walk it, Own it
By Meredith Coleman McGee
January 20, 2021

Don't talk about wealth inequality, talk about building wealth.
Don't talk about our former enslavement, talk about reparations.
Don't talk about systemic racism, build community institutions.
Don't talk about failing schools, create learning environments at home.
Don't talk about illiteracy, let's read.
Don't talk about the decline of the black press, subscribe.
Don't talk about overcrowded prison cans, free non-violent offenders.
Don't talk about poverty, create more opportunities.

Don't talk about urban decline, plan urban renewal.
Tell lawmakers to fix the streets and the infrastructure.
Let municipalities run at full employment.
Let counties run at full employment.
Outsourcing – forget about it!

Let's take selfies in black business districts.
Jose takes selfies in Hispanic business districts.
Bao takes selfies in Chinatown.
Let us shop at Jaquan's Book Hut around the corner.

Let empty commercial buildings in our hood warm laughing hearts.
Let empty commercial buildings in our hood accommodate shoppers.
Let empty commercial buildings in our hood employ our youth.
Let empty commercial buildings in our hood enlighten us.

Tell city leaders to tear down the plight.
Restore historical buildings.
Pick up the pieces left by the storm.
Revere the spirit of the rainbow.

I served as a judge of the youth contest. I read my newest poem *Talk it, Walk it, Own it* which I was inspired to write when Amanda Gorman read a poem during Pres. Biden's inauguration. As it turned out, this was the last event Will and I attended together and the first and last time Will heard me read the poem *Talk It, Walk it, Own It*.

The homeless are worth saving.
Establish public showers for the homeless.
Create jobs opportunities for the homeless.

Let's see new buildings going up.
Let's invest in valuable assets.

Support the fish fries, the candy lady, and the fruit stand.
Let us buy 1 home at a time - 1 business at a time.
Support neighborhood growth.
Support small. Support micro man!
There is a new business around the corner. Shop it.

Envision growth. Can you see it?
There is a Burger Rack where the abandoned building once stood.

There is hope where there was despair.
The people are taking selfies in black business districts.
Envision it! Can you see it?

Talk it, Walk it, Own it
By Meredith Coleman McGee
Pg. 2

We talked briefly to people on our way out of the park. Will and I went home, and he retired to our bed, got comfortable, and started flipping channels. I looked at him stretched across the bed with his head propped up on several pillows.

The next morning, which was Monday, Will stayed in bed longer than normal. I wasn't alarmed. I stayed close by. I went back and forth from my office and to daddy's room to check on him and to our room to check on Will. Daddy moved back in with us Aug 9, 2017, after his mother died. Will requested a few things. He watched his normal shows: Father Knows Best, Rifle Man, Leave it to Beaver... He was napping a little. I wasn't alarmed. I felt like he needed some rest.

His stepmom Betty called, and she asked, "Where Lil Will? I been calling him, and he isn't answering his phone." Will was four or so when Big Will started dating Betty. They married in 1971. Will was five and a half when Big Will married Betty. Betty dressed Will for Kindergarten. They had a great bond.

I replied he is sleep. Then she said, "Well if he sick, I'll come over there and help you take care of him. That's my boy."

I told her, "He's okay. I'll have him call you. Will doesn't answer the phone too quick if he is under the weather. Honestly, Will was sicker than I imagined. Eventually, he got up and left home for a few hours. Then, he returned and retired to our bed again. After I washed the dishes and took care of some things, I retired to our bed too. I walked from the bathroom to our bed. I noticed Will stretched out on the left side of the bed. I put his legs under the heating pad and turned it on to help ease the pain in his legs. We watched the news, nightline, and I found something on Netflix to watch.

Tuesday morning, June 1, 2021, Will stayed in bed again longer than normal. I fixed us something to eat and took his food to him. He didn't eat much. I gave him some yogurt, some water, and some cranberry juice. I have a habit of going to the restroom in our bedroom. When I passed by, Will sat up in the bed and he moved so his feet could hang off the bed; he grabbed me, hugged me tight, and he held on for several minutes.

A few minutes later I passed by again, Will sat up in the bed; his feet hung off the bed; he grabbed me, hugged me tight, and he held on. I went to my office, and I thought about the intensity of those hugs.

I walked back to our bedroom. Will sat up in bed; his feet hung off the bed; he grabbed me, hugged me tight, and he held on. I went to my office, and I thought about the force of those hugs. So, I started thinking something was strange.

I walked toward Will. He immediately sat up in the bed; his feet hung off the bed; he grabbed me, hugged me tight, and he held me.

By now, my mind was thinking about Mr. Pleasant, my step-grandfather in Buffalo. My grandmother Beulah told me Mr. Pleasant rushed to her bed to hug her the day he passed. He fell face down on their bed and died with his arms stretched out trying to hug her one more time. Now, I was alarmed, and wondering is this was such a day – a day where death was around the corner.

Will spoke to Short briefly and a few minutes later short pulled up. Spanky was with him. They drove the Maxima across the street to the vacant house under the Magnolia tree and Short took the struts off the car.

Will told me, "I'm going to the part store." I followed Will from our bedroom through the kitchen and through the living room. When he reached the door, he looked back and smiled. He said, "I'll be right back."

I stepped right behind him to see if he was okay. He waved his hand at me like go back. He walked outside on our small porch and then he stepped on the wheelchair ramp and held the ramp with his left hand. I stepped behind him. Then he looked back at me, smiled, and extended his elbow outward. I grabbed it and walked beside him to the car. I opened the car door. Will said, "I'll be back. I'm not going in. They are going in."

Short drove Will to see his Aunt Dorothy. She recalled Will squeezing her shoulder and saying, "I love you." She remembered that he always said, "The family needs to get together," referring to another family reunion and gathering.

Then, Short drove Will to Napa on Northside Drive to get struts for the Maxima. Will got out of the car and fell. Spanking and Short put Will in the car. Short drove Will to the ER at UMMC. Will's doctors are at St. Dominic. Short called me and told me he was on his way to get me because he had taken Will to the ER at the University. After he picked me up, we stopped by the part store, and I paid for the parts. He drove me to the ER and went back to the house and fixed the car. I kept asking to see Will, but they kept telling me to wait a few more minutes. I bugged the ER attendant. She kept calling in the back. A male ER doctor came out and asked me some questions. He told me to wait a few more minutes.

Several hours later a female doctor came out and asked my permission to put a ventilator on Will. I was allowed to see Will. His vitals looked good. His nurse told me they were taking him to ICU. I was told to return in the morning at 10 am. I felt Will's skin. I walked to his ear and whispered in it, "I love you." I was hopeful Will would pull through again. I grabbed his white tennis shoes off the floor and walked past the ER staff, through the double glass doors, down the sidewalk to the parking garage.

I went home and thought about Will in the hospital without me. I was eager for Tuesday to come so I could see Will. I knew he was going to want me there and I wanted to be there.

I watched the news and eventually fell asleep. Shortly after 12 midnight June 2, 2021, my phone rang which is a scary time for the phone to ring.

I said, "Hello."

The voice said, "I am doctor--. I have doctor --, doctor--, and doctor – on the line. We have done everything we can do but your husband is dying. You need to come quick."

I said, "Okay. I'm coming."

He asked, "How long will it take you to get here?"

"I live in south Jackson; I can be there in 15 minutes."

"Okay, I'll see what we can do. Hurry. Someone will meet you at the security desk."

I dressed in 60 seconds, grabbed my purse, got in the car, put the key in the ignition, crank the car up, and drove off.

I parked in the garage near the ER and walked briskly to the main entrance. I couldn't figure out how to ring the bell; so, I walked in behind an employee. The security guard stopped me and told me I couldn't enter.

I told the security guard the doctors called me and told me someone could meet me at the security desk. The guard called ICU, verified my story and someone walked down to the desk. He greeted me and I followed him.

When we reached the elevator he asked me, "Do you want to walk up the stairs or catch the elevator?"

"Walk up the stairs."

We walked up the stairs. I had been through those hospital doors many times. I had been outside those doors in a car while an aide pushed Will in a wheelchair from a hospital stay to our car or truck so I could take him home. He was always happy and smiling when he completed a hospital stay. We enjoyed our home and each other. But this day was not a good day. I was walking up the stairs, down that same hall, to that same ICU to talk to doctors about the love of life passing over leaving me here on this earth without him.

He led me to the first room on the left. Will was lying on his back. The staff described that he was in full life support. It took seven people to explain to me what was happening in this ICU room where Will was lying on a bed with a ventilator in his mouth. There were three of four machines around his body. There were tubes everywhere containing heart and resuscitation medication.

>Multisystem organ failure

>Lung vent breathing

>Kidney CRRT machine

I felt Will's feet and legs. They were warm. The nurse told me they had heating pads under Will. "Feel his head." I did. His temperature was 91. His head was on the cool side. His oxygen was 51. His breathing was 34. His blood pressure was dropping.

A voice said, "Sit down. His blood pressure is dropping." His blood pressure was 34 – 26.

I asked, "You mean it's going to be like on TV - Os – flat."

The voice said, "Yes. Have a seat."

I stood up and said, "No, I got to go. I can't stay here and watch that."

The male nurse said, "Okay I'll walk you down the security desk."

I walked to the left side of Will's hospital bed and whispered in his hear again, "I love you." The male nurse walked me down the hall pass the vending machines, to the elevator, down the stairs to the security desk. The security guard said something. I responded. Then, I walked down the hill. I had walked down that hill many times. I reached my car, got in, turned the ignition, crank the car, and drove off. I could barely see in front of me as I drove up State St. I don't know how I made it home, but I made it somehow. I parked the 2001 Maxima in the driveway behind the CTS Cadillac and my phone rang.

The voice said, "Your husband passed at 1:51 am. I'm sorry."

I told him, "Thank you."

Will succumbed to acute respiratory failure from the fungus on his left lung. By the time of his death there were three open cavities on his left lung.

I called Aunt Dorothy and my mother. My phone rang for days all day and through the night. I didn't sleep for the next 48 hours.

After 9am Tuesday morning June 2, 2021, a receptionist called and told me her office had gotten a referral for Will and was ready to make an appointment for his G.I. issues.

I blurted out, "He passed a few hours ago." She told me she was so sorry for my loss.

Cindy with Medicaid Waiver called, and I yelled, "My husband died." She gave me her sympathy.

I went to vote; we had been voting at precinct 68 for 22 years. I yelled, "I lost my husband." One of the poll workers walked from behind the counter and hugged me. The manager found Will's name on the list and marked it. I felt empty, lonely, and helpless. My neighbors came by and sat and talked with me.

Their company was extremely helpful. My sister purchased a ticket on the 2nd and by that Friday she arrived. My Aunt Mary volunteered to pick Eva up from the airport.

There were three phones constantly ringing. I answered Will's phone once. His Cousin Cherry called. I spoke to him. I walked on the porch and looked outside. I wondered how I would make it without Will. Brenda came by to check on me. My niece Christie called every morning. Moony called. Aunt Dorothy called. Ola Mae Called. Betty called. Many people called every day. The phones rang constantly. People called and gave so much praise on Will's character. I selected Willis and Sons to pick up Will's remains. They had handled Big Will's body.

The morning of June 3, 2021, I wrote a post on Facebook:

The post is below:

> Pinned Post
> Meredith McGee is with Adore Indy and 48 others at Meredith Etc · Jackson ·
> Shared with Public
> 🌐 June 3, 2021

I lost the love of my life yesterday. Thank you for your visits, calls, posts, prayers and well wishes. Tears. Missing you.

We got married in our backyard. We exchanged borrowed rings. He was a plumbing apprentice at South Central Heating and Plumbing. He and his supervisor did most of the pipe fitting for the bar @ Ameristar Casino.

He put together PCP piping, borrowed flowers from the church and made our wedding arc.

We jumped the broom like former slaves did because they couldn't get a marriage license.

Dwight borrowed ballroom chairs and tables from Holiday Inn where he was the food manager. Aunt Mary decorated. Aunt Chris cooked... Family pitched in.

Mama made my dress and hand stitched pearls on it. My stepmom videoed our day.

We made it work.
We had a love story made for books.
We went from $8 dollars an hour on up and went back down. Back Up.
Smiling now. My man. My love. My provider.

The post informed people of Will's passing. It was emailed to different people in various parts of the country. I received beautiful notes from strangers as well as from my friends in other states. Several widows who attended Callaway High School with Will talked to me via DM on Facebook. My former co-worker Aaron Hodge called daily. Will and I both spoke to Aaron the month before Will's passing. Aaron lost his wife in March of 2021. My insurance agent Clara saw the post and called. She gave me tips on how to handle the business of burying Will. Her tips were useful. Betty went with me to the funeral home to make Will's arrangements. She basically took charge. I told Betty I wanted Will's casket to match his sky blue and blue bow tie. Willis and Son did a fantastic job on Will. He looked like he was at peace. He died with a serene expression on his face.

When I saw that big smack of peace on Will's face, I imagined him embracing his Grandmother Christine, his Grandfather Leeandrew, Big Will, Ronnie, Fred, Mickey, Bro, Junior, Chris,

Dessa, Little, Fred, Lil Fred, Paul, Dwight, Duck, Craig, McGrew, Jeff... and so many others. I felt God ended Will's time on earth too suddenly. I wanted him back in my arms, in my space, in my face, in my presence. He remained in my head. His conversations were on my brain. I embraced his values, his hopes, his fears, his desire to be close to me. Life changed so quickly, so fast. One day I was a wife under the thump of my man. The next day I was alone, frightened, and crazy. Ties broke and people disappeared. I lost Will and gained Betty, Melvin, and 15 widows (one male, 14 females).

Rick called every day, "Girl you alright? You know Will was my buddy. Let Loretta help you do Will's funeral program.

"No, I'm not alright," I replied. "I am writing the obituary. I am going to try to set it up. I will call Loretta if I can't finish."

Rick called back, "You call Loretta?" So, I called. He was persistent. Rick called me every day for more than a week. I didn't run into any problems writing the obituary and doing the program. I had issues with the pictures. It was late so I didn't call Loretta who makes a living designing funeral programs. She is one of the best program designers in this city. I kept going. By June the 7th, I was in a bind. Brenda, BreeShae and Adarius came by. Brenda edited Will's funeral program and the three of them stayed up half the night folding his program. Eva stapled the programs. June 9th Wednesday morning, I took the programs to Willis and Sons so the funeral directors could pass them out at Will's graveside service.

That evening Michelle drove in from Aliceville, Alabama. She is a pastor and a friend of mine through the Rural Development Leadership Network. She joined the group of national leaders in 2012. Michelle was one of Will's angels when we were in New Mexico. She gave him some pain cream which really helped him so much. Michelle, Eva, and I sat in the living room and talked. I told them stories about Will and

Michelle had a few of her own. Michelle, Will, and I had been to several Assemblies together including the Assembly in North Carolina, NYC, North Georgia, Louisiana, New Mexico, and the three of us attended Billie Jean's 70th birthday celebration at Judson College in Marion, Alabama.

That night I slept at the foot of our bed on top of the covers. Will's heating pad was at the foot of our bed on his side. The white tennis shoes Will wore to the hospital June 1st were on the floor facing the gas space heater Will installed at least seven years ago. Years ago, he made me practice lighting the pilot and turning on the heater.

He told me, "You have to learn somethings, I might not be with you always."

"You might outlive me," I replied, "If you do, pay this house off and take care of yourself."

Will told me over the years, "I would rather leave here before you or Dew."

I had not considered life without Will. My life as a widow has not been a bed of roses. I've walked on thorns since Will passed. They say time heals all wounds. But how much time? Grief is different for everyone. Losing my spouse was a ton of bricks. It was worse than losing my brothers, my grandparents, my stepfather. I had never known such pain. It is piercing deep.

CHAPTER 5
Graveside

Wednesday the 9th, Will's public viewing was at Willis and Sons on Robinson Road extension about 1.5 miles from our home. I arrived about 1:30pm and placed flyers announcing the time and location of Will's graveside service so visitors could take one home. Most viewers took a flyer and signed his book. The flyer is below.

William Earl McGee Jr.

Sunset, Wed. June 2, 2021, age 55

Public viewing Wed. June 9, 2021, 1pm – 6pm
Willis & Sons Funeral Home
5235 Robinson Rd. Extension
Jackson, MS 39204

Graveside Service Thur. June 10, 2021: 11 am
Autumn Woods Cemetery
4000 W. Northside Dr.
Jackson, MS 39209
601.353.3482

There were three couches in the room where Will was lying in state. My Aunt Mary and Aunt Judy arrived and sat with me for a while which was very comforting. Ms. Earnestine, Ms. Bee, Aunt Glenn, Mischa, Umekia, JaQuana, Melvin,

Jackie, Uncle J-Boy, Jessica, and many people from Shady Oaks and people who attended Brinkley Middle School and Callaway High School with Will paid respects to Will as he was lying in state.

Ma' Melvin was grieving pretty bad. Ant was torn up. I tried to help his wife comfort him. I call him "Lil Bro." Will called him "Young Buck." Ant and Will did plumbing jobs together for years. Will and McGrew helped Ant get on in the plumbing department at JSU. I went home at 5:40 pm. I didn't get the opportunity to greet everyone who attended Will's viewing. I was there to greet most viewers.

Ladarius told me, "I arrived a few minutes after 6. They had closed the door. I asked Mr. Willis to please let me in to see my friend." Mr. Willis unlocked the door and let Ladarius pay his respects to Will.

Ladarius said, "Man! Get up from there!" Ladarius told me Will looked like he was asleep. He did. Oh' my God Will looked good. I touched his wavy hair and popped him on his stomach several times.

I was happy people came to pay respects to Will. Will was the most important person in my life. He was number one. No one was above him. Will always declared, "I don't play second base." Will was my King! His was black, handsome, loving, gentle, brilliant man. Someone told me I put Will on a pedestal. I did. Cloud nine. I am keeping his memory going. His good legacy is important to me. He put me on a pedestal. Yes. I did.

One day in May Will told me, "I am not afraid to die."

"Why you say that?" I asked.

"I'm just telling you. I am not afraid to die. I had a good life.

I had a great life with you." I understood him. But I was not alarmed. I felt life would continue.

The morning of June 10th, I prepared breakfast for my house guest and went about the business of dressing for Will's graveside service. Eva took my hair loose and redid it. I put on a white dress and my sister insisted it was not appropriate to wear to Will's homegoing. So, I put on a blue dress which matched the color in Will's sky blue and blue casket. Eva and Michelle were pleased with the second dress. The last time I wore that dress Will wore his favorite blue suit which was March of 2020 to Respect Our Black Dollars banquet at the Masonic Temple on Lynch Street down the street from JSU. I remember Will trying on his suit to wear afterward but he couldn't button it up. So, he picked another suit. I had dressed Will in one of his black suits. Poncho wanted his big brother buried in his favorite suit, but I had other plans for the blue suit.

The limousine driver pulled in front of the house at 10:30 pm. His vehicle could hold four people comfortably. A few cars pulled up to follow the limousine to Autumn Woods Memorial Gardens Cemetery. Will's Uncle Michael, Aunt Sharon, cousins Jeffery and Spanky were outside in parked vehicles. Michelle followed us too. She planned to drive back to Aliceville, Alabama after the graveside service was over. I spoke to everyone seated in their cars.

The limousine driver opened the door and Eva, and I got in. As we turned the corner onto Maria Drive, the grief hit me like a ton of bricks. I was in the air feeling lost and empty. It was unbelievable eight days after Will's passing, we were laying him to rest which was eight months after we laid Big Will to rest. I purchased a double burial plot with Will's money June 7, 2021, so, I could be buried next to him when my time came. Will died with good credit and at a time when his goal was saving money and paying cash when possible. We were paying extra on our mortgage to pay it off in 34 months. Our goal was being debt-free like some members of Heirs United Investment Club.

Program

Thursday, June 10, 2021 Graveside Service 11:00 a.m.
Autumn Woods Cemetery, 4000 W. Northside Dr. Jackson, MS 39209

Prayer	Pastor Elizabeth McGee, widow of Fred McGee
Scripture Old Testament	Pastor Patricia Williams
Scripture New Testament	Pastor Patricia Williams
Reading of the Obituary	Vickie Robinson
Reading of Poems/Cards	Vickie Robinson
Prayer/Eulogy	Phillip K. Reed, Minister
	New Horizon Church International
Words of Expression	Dorothy McGee, Aunt
Song ....*Peace of Mind*	Dorothy McGee
Words of Expression cont.	Curtis McGee, Uncle
	Michelle Cole Barnes, Friend
	Karen Smith, Sister
Family & Friends (3 minutes)	open
Song	Tammy Litt
Song	Linda Purvis
Closing remarks	Dorothy McGee, Aunt
Willis & Sons Funeral Directors in charge	
Recession	
Peace be with you while we are absent one from another	

Family time is special anytime! All the way up!

I didn't talk during the ride to the cemetery. I looked out the window. I was in shock and in disbelief because I was in a limousine wearing a blue dress to go take a front seat at Will's graveside service. The route the limousine driver took was a route Will and I drove many times. The driver drove up Highland Dr. to Lynch St. to Hwy 80 pass Metro Mall through side streets including Loflin St. and Dixon Rd to Northside Dr.

When we reached the cemetery, it was drizzling and raining. Dozens of people were holding umbrellas. Everything about the scene appeared like a big blur. I passed by people; my mind was blank. I remember Short's sister extending her hand to help me. She told me several people had already fallen, and she didn't want me to fall. After she mentioned people falling, I held her hand and proceeded with caution. I sat in a seat on the front row in front of Will's two-toned blue casket. "Mr. William E. McGee Jr" was engraved on the casket in gold letters in the center at the bottom. Around eight of the chairs under the tarp were empty. A few minutes later a few people sat in the chairs.

For the most part the program was carried out. Will's younger sister Karen declined to speak but her brother-in-law, Pastor Smith spoke on her behalf. He mentioned meeting Will at her wedding in March of 2019. I put the picture of Will walking Karen down the aisle to marry Russell in Will's funeral program. Karen told me that was one of the most momentous events in her life and she was so proud her 'big brother' walked her down the hall on her special day. Will's Uncle Curtis did not speak and the two people who agreed to sing did not sing. Other than that, everyone who was supposed to be on the program participated.

Vickie read my love poem *15 Years With Will* which I wrote on our 15th Wedding anniversary in 2014. Two of the lines were omitted from the funeral program. Khadiya said when

15 Years With Will

By Meredith Coleman McGee, Sept. 25, 2014 (*15th wedding anniversary poem*)

Twenty-three years ago we laid eyes on one another
for the first time.

Fifteen years ago we jumped the broom in the presence of our
family and friends.

Seventeen years ago we danced slow—like it wasn't
nobody's business.

We danced in the living room; we dance by our bed; we danced
in the hall.

We danced off the wall. We had a ball, by our lonesome selves.

This morning I woke up and saw your handsome face.

I knew then, it was going to be a super awesome day.

You were sleeping peacefully waiting to greet me.

The day was going to be joyous because we have each other.
The day is going well because we love one another.

Our life together has been blessed because we have each other's back.

I held your hand when you needed me.
You rubbed my feet when they ached.
We made it.
Even when others put obstacles in our way, we survived it.
We conquered those days.
We survived even when one of us faltered or failed.
We love deeper. Thank you for true love.
Live the skyline above. Blue, sparkling with rays. Happy days.
Your love is like a flower.
It blooms; it shines; it spread its wings; it catches my attention.
You are wonderful. You are exceedingly fine—like red wine.
Tingly. Tang' Wang' Thang.'
You are my sunshine. You are my moonlight...
I need your smile in my face. I need you. I love you. Thank you.
Tingly. Tang' Wang' Thang' Hmm.

I read it at our 20th wedding anniversary, "Oh, I can't believe she's reading that X-rated poem."

Traa was not on the program. I invited him to speak. He said, "I think I will." He walked up and spoke well. Traa told the audience that Will was still with us in our hearts, in our memories, and in pictures. He was telling the truth. A framed picture of Will at age 34 is on the bookshelf in my home office. He was posing near a display in the middle of the floor at the Aviation Museum in Pensacola, Florida wearing a Hawaii patterned light green short sleeve shirt, smiling deeply, with his hands in his pocket.

A paper picture of us in the History Museum after we toured the new Mississippi Civil Rights Museum on North St. is taped on the closet door. My favorite museum in the City of Jackson is the Smith Robertson Museum. Junior attended the Smith Robertson School in the 50s. My brother Bobby attended in 1970-1971 - the year it closed.

I asked Will earlier this year, "What is your favorite book written by your wife?"

"Nashida: Visits the Smith Robertson Museum," Will replied. That was news to me. I'm so glad I asked.

The funeral director opened the casket after Traa spoke. I stood up, walked to the casket, and rubbed Will's hair and patted his stomach. Jeffery and Will's younger brother Rashad walked to the casket to get a close view. My cousin Charlet was breathing hard and whelping. Will's biological mother, Melvin Nichols, was sitting in the center in one of the extra chairs behind the 12 chairs placed under the tarp by the funeral home directors. Betty was not far away. The two women did not know each other.

I was Will's legs on Mother's Day, Sunday, May 9, 2021. He was not feeling good that day. He told me he wanted to go out for a minute. I volunteered to drive him as I knew he was not feeling his best. He had already purchased me two flower plants and placed the plants on our porch.

Will told me to go in the store and find two bouquets of flowers. I did. I drove him to his mother's apartment on Robinson Road. We got out and she told me to go in the kitchen, get a knife, cut the stems lower and place her flowers in a vase on her kitchen sink. She was pleased to see Will. We talked for a while. She complained about an ailment and Will told her not to worry and declared, "I got you Ma'." Mother and son had taken another step. Will acknowledged his mother on Mother's Day with flowers.

His grandmother Christine taught Will many things. One thing Will said she always said was, "Give me my flowers while I'm living." A gift of flowers from Will was a significant gesture. When I was helping Will raise his son, Will planted my flowers in the dirt in front of our house every year for Mother's Day.

We went by my mother's house. I gave her a gift. Will told her "Happy Mother's Day." She thanked him. We talked with mama a few minutes. Then, we left to go to Betty's house off Capital St.

Will called Betty and asked, "You at home?"

She said, "I'm here."

"Your boy is on his way," Will said.

I pulled the car in front of her house. Will and I walked in. Betty told me to lay the flowers on the table. She hugged Will, smiled, and thanked him for her flowers. He had purchased her flowers many times over the years. She had been in his life since he was four years old. She attended Will's high school graduation from Callaway H.S. with Big Will, Christine McGee, and Dorothy McGee. Betty spent time with us on our wedding day. Her younger brother Danny and Will were playmates growing up.

At the end of Will's Graveside service, the rain subsided, and various people tapped me on the shoulder or hugged me. I spotted Uncle Butch standing near his car and rushed to greet him. I had driven Will to his house on May the 27th. They talked so long, I went in the kitchen and got on the phone and let them have it.

I wanted to stay at Will's grave longer. But the limousine driver was rushing me. My nephew D.D. had taken my purse and my African American Family Heirloom Bible and put it on the back seat of the limousine. My family was taking care of me.

D.D. told me, "I got you Auntie."

The ride from the cemetery home was as difficult as the ride had been from our home to the cemetery. I looked out the window and thought about the decades Will and I had spent together. We had travelled on Northside Dr. and Country Club Blvd. and Hwy. 80 and J.R. Lynch St. over the years in a 1996 Toyota Camry, in a 1979 Dodge, in three different F-150 trucks, in a 2001 Nissan Maxima, and in a 2004 CST Cadillac.

I thought about the lyrics of the poem *The unwatered plant* I wrote years ago:

She gave up the ghost.

They dressed in black and rode in that pretty Cadillac.

She is no more.

They all cried at her graveside.

Here I was riding in a pretty Cadillac because I had just overseen the burial of the one man who loved me 23 years and four months. My feelings were all over the place. I wanted Will back. I saw him looking good in his black suit and the multi-colored blue bow tie. I heard him when I looked at the peace on his face; he was happy in heaven. I heard him; but I couldn't stop longing for his presence. Don't get me wrong, I appreciated 23 years and four months of true love. Regardless of imperfection, Will and I loved each other deeply. No man ever loved me so passionately and so deliberately. Will felt the same sentiments of me.

Will's love poured out like a river. His devotion was deeper than anger, deeper than yelling, it was purer than a misunderstanding. His love was real. I felt his love when he reversed an unwise decision, when he travelled with me regardless of his physical pain, when he honored the people I honored, when he did everything in his power to celebrate me and us.

Will proudly wore his 'Buffalo Bills' baseball caps and sweatshirts as proudly as he wore Las Vegas apparel. Grandma Beulah was a diehard Buffalo Bills fan. Will carried his leather Tuskegee case like a badge of honor. He wanted to be wherever I was. I wanted to be wherever he was. If Will wanted me to watch *Father Knows Best*, I gladly listened to him discuss Kathy and Bud.

His YouTube playlist included music by "Mystical, Public Enemy, James Brown, Pac, Snoop, NWA, Christ Brown, Chance the Rapper, Kevin Gates, Boosie, 2 Chainz, UGK, Canton Spirituals, Soul Stirrers, DMX, Young Thug, DaBaby, T.I., Rick Ross, Yo Gotti, Rich Homie Quan, Lil

Wayne... We are proud of David Banner, the most famous rapper and actor from Mississippi. We shared great pride in seeing David Banner on the silver screen. Will said, "David Banner use to be in Battlefield Park. Look at him now."

In seven days, I wrote Will's obituary, found pictures for his program, cancelled his doctor appointments, washed his dirty clothes, and walked through a house he ruled and greeted his spirit from the front to the back, from the yard to the street – in the chair, on the couch, in the kitchen, in my office, in the den, and in the wind. Will, Will, Will!

I miss Will every day. There were three repast services honoring Will. I hosted family, neighbors, and friends at our house. The food was catered and sponsored by one of our mutual friends. We enjoyed it. Will's sister next to him Michelle hosted the family at her home which she shared with her husband Kevin. Will's mother Melvin hosted a repast at her apartment.

My immediate family including my cousin Gordie and friends were at our home. Mr. Govan and his daughter attended the repast at our home. Mae Ma stopped by and brought a cake. Everyone's presence was very comforting to me. Gordie kept us rolling with jokes. My Aunt Judy said, "I told Will his repast food is delicious." Traa stopped by and greeted everyone and used his cell phone and took pictures of pictures around the wall. I gave Traa his dad's favorite blue suit. He was so happy to have it. He tried it on, and he said it fit him perfectly.

I unwillingly entered a new chapter in my life, becoming a 57-year-old widow. I had a rocky transition from being under the thumb of my husband to being a widow. I was blessed with family and friends. But making decisions on repairs without Will and outside of his circle was hard.

CHAPTER 6
The Widow

Every Inch Love Will

After Eva flew back to Georgia, me and daddy were the only occupants of the house. Daddy's nurse came during the day. After that the loneliness which plagues a widow sat there and didn't want to leave. I kept moving. That Saturday, June 12, 2021, I picked up Betty and my cousin Charlet and they accompanied me to the *Stand Up, Speak Up: Rally 4 Peace* at Flowers Park. Will made the first investment in the rallies by purchasing a tailgate speaker to accommodate the open mic process.

We attended the rally and at one point I got very emotional at the mic. I missed Will so much. His absence hurt so badly. I took Betty and Charlet home and didn't put enough water in the radiator. The car stopped in the middle of J.R. Lynch St. off Hwy. 80. I was afraid for my safety. My lights were not on. The car was dead. I was in a hazardous spot with heavy traffic. I couldn't call Will. I called Unc. next door. He came but it was too hard for him to get to my car. An older lady pulled her car in front of me and turned her lights on. Her teenage grandson was trying to help too.

She asked me, "What's wrong with your car."

I told her, "It ran hot and stopped."

She told me to pop the hood. I popped the hood. She told me the car was really hot. She poured water on the motor.

She asked me, "This how you operate baby? You get up and put water in the car. You got to get this fixed. You in a bad spot you can get hurt out here."

Her words stung me like a bee. I knew then I was vulnerable. I thought about it and reasoned that Will had been vulnerable too. He was getting up every day putting water in the radiator. Everything was piling up repair wise. He had fixed several things around the house; he was trying to fix the cars. He started slowing down in 2021. He did one or two things per day. Then, he retired to our bed.

A police officer came; the woman (an angel) spoke with her and told her I needed a boost off. The officer said she didn't have any booster cables. A few minutes later another officer came; he had cables. The woman and he poured water in the radiator. She made a U-turn in the street and drove her car to face my car. She and the male officer put the cables on my car and her car and waited a few minutes; after several attempts to charge my battery, the car started.

I was so happy and grateful for this angel and those police officers. After my car ran a minute, the woman hit the hood of my car with her hand and told me, "Go. Go."

I pulled off and waved. Unc. followed me. I made it home and set out to fix the cars. There was so much wrong with the Maxima. Only one out of the four black males, mechanics was fair. This chapter in my life was so foreign. Will had always taken care of car and home repairs. Things had piled up on him at the end. In April of 2021, Will installed a new water heater and had tree limbs cut; he had Spanky put new sheetrock in the storage house, and had some woodwork repaired. Our home and car projects were a work in progress.

I told Ladarius, "Many black men have no respect for black women."

He replied, "Some of them don't have respect for black men either." He told me he experienced shady mechanic dealings too. In general, the widows I talked with felt men in general respect men more than they respect women.

Brenda told me I had been privileged for years to have a husband because what I experienced after Will closed his eyes was the norm for single women. I felt like I had been punched in the face. She made light of it.

Will had said, "The Maxima don't owe us nothing." The Maxima was riding good in 2019. When you don't nip things in the bud, they get out of hand. After Will's Graveside, Ms. Irma told me about a mechanic on Terry Rd. She drove me to his house. There were five or six cars in his yard. I couldn't distinguish which ones belonged to him or which ones he was working on.

Anyway, he told me he would give me a deal. His deal involved me giving him money upfront and him repairing the car the following day.

I told him, "I ain't never gave no one any money upfront.

He said, "I'm giving you a deal. He asked, "You gone give me the money?"

I told the mechanic, "I can buy the part now and pay the labor when you finish." He slammed the door in my face.

Ms. Irma said, "He slammed the door. I'm sorry. I didn't know he was gonna' act like that. Someone told me about him. I'm going to tell my old man about this. We're not going to use him."

"What you want to do now?" Ms. Irma asked.

"Let's go to AutoZone."

Ms. Irma drove me to AutoZone. I walked to the counter, and I asked the clerk if he could give me a referral for a mechanic because my car was running hot. A man was in the line behind me. The clerk asked him if he could help me. He said he could help. I drove the car to his shop, and he stopped it from running hot, but it stopped after I drove it 3 miles. I called him and he and another man drove where I was, and Ms. Irma came and picked me up to take me home.

He kept the car two weeks, so I asked Spanky to go with me to pick up the car. Spanky told me not to drive it anymore until I fixed it. In the end, I was without transportation for eight weeks. My circle got smaller. Aunt Mary came several times and took me to the grocery store. Calla took me places when she was not fixing hair. Shirley drove from Florida and stayed with us four or five days. I used her car when she was in Jackson. My female neighbors did the rest. Nicole and Odetta took me to the dollar store, to the grocery store and Odetta's husband loaded his three young children on the back seat and drove me to 90.1 for a radio interview one night.

During the first week of July, I picked up the car from another shop. While standing outside waiting on AAA, I saw a cat walking across the field clutching the center of a live rat between its teeth. The rat's tail and hind legs were hanging down. The cat walked slowly and confidently out of my view in a ditch with its captive.

There I stood, cell phone in one hand, fingers busy, mind full, posting pictures sharing my Facebook status, not sure if the truth was as important as the picture of my car parked kissing the steel edges of the exterior of a mechanic shop.

I thought to myself - my husband is gone. He is not here. He left me, not intentionally. His maker called him home. I was not ready for his transition. I want him back. My current situation was anything but pleasant. I was walking through another unsuccessful car repair situation waiting on the tow truck. Thirty minutes passed. One hour passed. The mail carrier had completed her route in that section and was passing by again. It was hot. I was so thirsty. I stopped her and asked the sister if she had any water.

She told me, "You could have asked me when you saw me at first. Then she smiled and handed me a cold bottle of water.

"Thank so much!" I said humbly. She smiled, giving me a renewed sense of hope.

One hour and a half passed. Finally, the tow truck arrived. I was happy to be getting out of Dodge City. As Will would say, "I was ready to go to the Ponderosa."

Every Inch Love Will, a memoir about my late husband grew out of my pain. I had initially shared my loss publicly through my Facebook status, June 3, 2021.

When I fell in love with Will, I was an avid reader. Eight years later I submitted *The Stranger's Spring,* a poem inspired by him, for publication; it was my first published poem. Three years later, I co-authored *Married to Sin.* I transferred myself into a book publisher in 2013. Will supported my career moves. He became a plumber and never switched fields. He loved his trade. Wife, son, family, friends, plumbing, community, football, basketball...

During my isolation I wrote Will's memoir. Within two weeks, I wrote 20,000 words. By the fourth week I had written **40,211 words.** I had never written so much so fast in my life. *Every Inch Love Will* is Will's memoir and a love story. Writing about our love affair was a very emotional roller coaster. "Sugar Foot sang, "Roller Coaster, your love.

Say what." As things progressed and the word count increased, I started feeling a sense of accomplishment and drew inspiration from his story.

My sister Eva said of my writing feat, "Your adrenaline kicked in." It did. The storytelling unfolded as I typed into the computer keyboard with Will's spirit soaked in my soul.

A writer asked me, "Are you writing a journal or a book?"

"I'm writing a book for the market."

Lynette told me to discuss what it's like to be a widow. Well, being a widow was a tough cookie for me because I wanted to grow old with my husband. We had daily, weekend, and annual routines. We had unfulfilled plans. When Will passed, I was traumatized. I didn't sleep for 48 hours. My sleep patterns changed. I slept less and roamed the house.

I asked myself 50 times, "What is this?" My husband is not here in the room I shared with him for 22 years and 10 months. He was not here yesterday, the day before that, and the day before that. His absence is not normal.

I couldn't trust people I thought I could trust, and I trusted people I shouldn't have. Overall, I received great advice. Hearing stories from other widows was especially important. My Aunt Mary gave me great advice too. She told me grieving women can get in trouble easily. She told me she knew women who became widows and were taken over by alcohol or went through men. She told me vulnerable people can get lost. She told me there is a grieving period. It takes time. Everyone grieves differently. "You can't rush the process of healing," Aunt Mary declared.

Meredith S. Coleman & William E. McGee Sat. 09. 25. 1999

Betty and Melvin stuck with me too. I had a great support system. People could hear pain in my voice. My dad's nurse asked a counselor from the VA to check on me. He called me and set up a grief counseling session. He spoke with daddy first who lived with us. Then, he told me Ms. Mabel told him I lost my husband, and he was concerned about me. I sat in the white chair, and he sat in the flowered chair in the living room.

He asked me, "So, tell me about your relationship with your husband."

"We had a great relationship. We enjoyed travelling, movies, dining out, cooking together... we enjoyed each other's company..." I replied.

He told me, "Oh' that's bitter and it's sweet." He added, "Grief is like a war wound. The more you love the person the harder it is for the wound to heal. I counsel widows who are happy to get rid of their spouses. Their wound heals faster."

My friend Ella, who attended Utica Junior College with me 1981-1983 counseled me too. She met Will at the *Stand Up, Speak Up: Rally 4 Peace* at Grove Park on Parkway Ave in Shady Oaks May 22, 2021. Ella told me she knew immediately Will was my husband because we were wearing matching t-shirts displaying the Meredith Etc Cash App. Ella moved over so Will could sit beside me.

"Meredith got to be your wife. You sit beside her," Ella told Will.

"'That's my sweet thang'," Ella said, Will declared.

Ella moved over and Will sat beside me. He was happy to oblige her. He was dog sitting for Pastor Patricia Williams that day. Will enjoyed walking the dog around.

Ella counseled me four or five evenings in a row. Everything positive was helpful.

One night, as I sat on the porch alone, a new ritual, to take a break from the house, an owl perched on the light pole near the left side of our house next to unc's driveway. The owl turned its head around and looked in my direction. Then, it flew away. Will and I had been looking for that owl for years. The sight of the owl was a sign of good fortune. Keshia, a new friend, who is also a widow told me "God favors orphans and widows. The owl was confirmation.

One day I went in daddy's room, and he asked me, "Where is your husband?"

I said, "He is in heaven."

Daddy replied, "No he ain't."

I said, "Well where is he?"

Daddy said, "He's back. Look behind you."
I looked behind me at daddy's clothes in the closet and his 2021 wall calendar and wondered how daddy knew Will had

returned. Will's presence comforted me. One widow told me her husband's spirit stayed in the home they shared 40 years for 60 days.

July 15, 2021, I gave up on the Maxima and focused on repairing the Cadillac. There were serious issues with it too. In 2020 Will gave in to Ice T's CarShield propaganda and purchased CarShield. Unfortunately for us, dealerships in Jackson do not accept CarShield. Two complained of slow payments. I don't think dealerships are interested in repairing older model cars. Nissan service was the same way. One day the manager told me my car was too old to enter his service center.

I told him, "I bought it out there (pointing at the parking lot full of new Nissan vehicles)."

He told me, "I'll run a diagnosis on it and tell you what's wrong with it."

On my birthday, July 20th, I had the Cadillac towed to the Cadillac dealership. They repaired one issue and kept the car on the grounds three weeks. Will and I had taken the Cadillac to a white owned shop on Hwy. 80 around February of 2021; according to the Cadillac dealership the previous mechanics put the wrong spark plugs in the car and damaged the motor. I didn't trust that prognosis. I experienced shady dealings with people of all races this year. Aunt Mary told Uncle Claudel about my car repair drama. He picked me up and drove me to the dealership to look under the hood and speak with the technician. He advised me not to go any further with the Cadillac. I had spent $2,300 and the bill was getting fatter - obese.

Uncle Claudel advised me to consider starting over and getting a Hyundai, taking care of it, and keeping it 20 years like we kept the Maxima. He told me Hyundai's were well-built and cheaper to maintain than luxury cars, Hondas, Nissans, and Toyotas. I got a box and removed my items from the Cadillac. I asked an employee in service to loan me a Phillip head screwdriver to remove the front and rear tag plates. The employee removed the tags. I cleared the glove department out and removed items from the trunk.

Two days later, on the 19th of August, Uncle Claudel took me car shopping and I was driving a new Hyundai Sonata with a warranty. I know Will is happy I can touch the car with my finger, and it unlocks. He used to be concerned that I waited to find my car keys when I reached the car, which took too long. "Have you keys out before you get to the car," he complained.

My traumatic experience had different lives. Holidays, closing accounts, and other things triggered my grief. Widows understood my strange behavior. I walked at night looking through windows, was paranoid and insecure. Every day was a new day in my life as a widow. I lost my husband. He was 55. I became a 57-year-old widow. I thought 100's of times: Will is not here. He is gone from this earth. I lost the love of my life and a big chunk of my heart, June 2, 2021.

I felt his death over and over. Deleting my deceased husband from our car insurance, learning that the motor was gone 07.15.2021 in the Maxima at 3pm on Hooker St. E-signing the form to delete the Maxima from the car insurance, deleing my husband as an occupant of our home. I had to remove my husband from the business accounts. Mercy! The grief revisited me with a vengeance.

My husband was not there to buy me a package of ground turkey, or to smile at me, or to pat me on the shoulder or my behind. He was gone. I received 42 sympathy cards, dozens of email notes, and 100's of phone calls.

Hinds County Tax Collector Eddie Fair and Hinds County Supervisor David Archie presented resolutions to the family on behalf of our loss of William Earl McGee Jr. Jackson Advocate newspaper which was my highest paid job after college published Will's obituary. Those acts of kindness were very uplifting. I framed Will's newspaper clipping on the right side of Leeandrew McGee's WWII original official photograph. I framed and hung the two resolutions in our den below Big Will's and Will's newspaper clippings.

Mr. Archie, slightly older than Will, grew up in Shady Oaks. Mr. Fair is related to one of our nations most heralded Folk Sheroes Fannie Lou Hamer. I showed the wall of fame to Jeffery McGee. He said proudly looking at his grandfather, uncle, and cousin, "This is like a museum."

Will told me often, "The first thing I see every morning is granddaddy's picture." Leeandrew was a shining example of manhood. He encouraged Will's work ethics and inspired Will's entrepreneurial spirit. Will earned money mowing lawns at age 10 and later had a newspaper route for the Clarion Ledger; he and his friends walked to the stadium to work in his preteen years. Will bragged about the tips they received at Ole Miss and Mississippi State games. The late City Councilman Frank Bluntson once told Will, "Your grandfather was one of my greatest mentors."

Will's June Social Security check was the end of the row. The cash and checks from the sympathy cards totaled $1,720.00. The funds were helpful. I had tree limbs cut which damaged our roof, paid to have wood replaced in the back of the house, and paid to have trash removed. I installed security measures such as outside lighting, paid for extensive yard work...

I watched a comedy show for the first time without Will featuring Chappelle on Netflix October 6, 2021. Will loved Chappelle. Chappelle made a joke about being the guy who got off a bus and left $50,000 on it. Will and I were sitting in our den watching the Chappelle Show faithfully when Chappelle walked away from his show. I laughed without Will four months and four days after Will closed his eyes.

Before the Thanksgiving Holiday, Eva mailed me some beautiful pieces of jewelry. My new pieces and the pieces I accumulated from Will in recent years was a lot. So, I ordered a large jewelry box. Little by little I placed the matching earrings in the compartments. On the eve of Thanksgiving, I cleaned my dresser top and in the back was a 14K gold Herringbone necklace.

I knew immediately Will purchased it before he passed because no one on this earth except him knows where I keep my loose costume jewelry which I wear from day to day. During 2020, Will and I went to a jeweler to get a stone replaced in one of my rings and I admired the necklaces in the glass case.

I pointed at several items and asked, "How much is that?"

"This one?"

"Yes."

"$$$."

"Oh!" We couldn't afford nothing in that case.

Janice told me, "It was meant for you to find this necklace at this time because you are struggling with your loss. Not many people experience long love. You were blessed to share a long love."

Look at God. A new sign of Will's love appeared the same month I purchased a blue stoned forever necklace for $34.00. I love this necklace too. Blue has a special meaning relating to Will.

Betty said, "Maybe Lil Will was going to surprise you for your birthday."

The necklace was a sign of good fortune. I realize fortune is defined differently for all of us. Will and I moved in our home six months after we met, and we married one year and a half after we danced in a hole in the wall. One day before we married, I told Will, "You're the last cowboy."

Fri. Dec. 10, 2021, Vickie and I saw Eddie Griffin at Chuckles Comedy House. I believe Will and I saw Eddie Griffin at the Coliseum a few years ago. Eddie Griffin made a statement which really stuck with me. He said when he was growing up his mother would wait on the porch for him to return home but today mother's let their children stay out all night. They don't enforce rules like 'be home before the streetlights come on.' He hit the nail on the head with that revelation. Children need law and order at home. I enjoyed the show and felt Will's presence riding back home. We went everywhere together as a couple. Will was always there to accompany me to events. I miss him.

Starry emailed my Facebook post from June 3rd to people she knows in our national network. Most of the people she emailed knew me, but some did not. I would have given the world to get Will back. One day, I re-read my notes. I was reminded Will never left me. He is here!

    Email notes:

As I think upon your loss, and is it really? for his spirit will be with you where ever you go, his touch, his smell, will always be there, for those things have become a part of you over the years, how wonderful is our maker, that he makes it possible for us to think, remember, and with our minds spirit ourselves away to those places that only you and Will knew. Bless you my sister I do not know you, but I can feel your pain. Your picture of your wedding and the arch that Will made especially for you, what a blessing... Rest my sister for he is with you until you and he meet again. In Jesus all is at rest...

Margarita, Dade City, Florida

Meredith, I am so saddened by your loss of Will. Please, I know it is a crazy request because of distance, but if I can help in any way – let me know.

You two were my ideal couple; you had such a strong bond and for people like myself, that was my takeaway treasure after each visit with you both.

Love you, take care

Twila, North Dakota

Dearest Meredith,

So, many times I've thought of you and your fine hubby Will. Always very pleasant memories. There are people who pass through our lives who leave a happy memory. Will was such a person!

Take care of yourself.

Till we meet again.

Twila, North Dakota

- - - - - - - - - - - - -

Hi Meredith,

I am feeling your sorrow and know that you are in pain over losing Will, your husband and best friend. Think of all the many good moments you had together and know that he is with you. He was always there at every meeting and during our activities. I feel he was your rock, and you were his rock.

One day, those rocks will join again.

Love,

Shirley Sherrod, Albany, Georgia

- - - - - - - - - - - - -

Hi cousins,

I happened to call Meredith McGee yesterday and she told me that her husband Will had just died earlier that morning!

He was a wonderful man, and so very supportive of our family connections. Will, we will miss you!

Rest in Peace.

Susanne Lowe, great, great granddaughter of Josiah Abigail Patterson Campbell, Chief Justice, Mississippi Supreme Court, 1876-1894

Note: Meredith is a Black great, great granddaughter of JAP Campbell. Will and Meredith hosted a picnic for JAP Campbell's Black and White descendants on April 24, 2021. JAP Campbell owned Minnie Brown and was the father of Francis Brown, mother of Moses (Cap) Arthur Meredith. Cap was Meredith's grandfather. His picture is in our den next to Will's great grandmother Sara Travis McGee.

I made an appointment with Social Security in August to obtain the $250.00 which Social Security gives to widows. At the end of the appointment, the representative told me to call back when I turned 59 and seven months so I could apply for Survivors Social Security and since Will had only been married previously three years, I will be the only spouse to draw his funds. Oh my God. If I live that long, I will be eligible as his widow to receive ¾ of his check at age 60 and 100% of it when I turn 67. So far, I belong to William Earl McGee Jr. No other man has touched me. His words are in my head. His love is sealed in my heart.

Usually, Will and I plant green, red, and yellow bell peppers, jalapeno peppers, cherry tomatoes, and regular tomatoes every spring. The only plant which bloomed this spring was the jalapeno pepper plant, but we didn't plant anything else. By the 9th of October I decided to keep our potted garden tradition going and I planted cabbage and buttercrunch lettuce.

Cabbage, top plant, buttercrunch lettuce, bottom plant

Billie Jean Young's 70 Birthday Celebration, Marion, AL
Picture of the late icon Fannie Lou Hamer on the table
Photo William and Meredith McGee Family Collection

Will in a gift shop in Biloxi, Mississippi. Will drove
Meredith & William Trest to a TV appearance at WLOX

I recently found a card from Will honoring 19 years of marriage with me. He wrote, "19 years - my beautiful wife" at the top of the card. The printed note on the card said, "There may be other fish in the sea... But not for me. Happy Anniversary." He signed the card, "Love you, today, tomorrow, and forever."

I smile now thinking about the day I saw Will at the 900 Club shooting pool wearing that light blue denim outfit, muscles flexing, skin shining, waiting for an old man to fall asleep so he could get the girl of his dreams.

He got me. We did that baby. We loved strong and hard for 23 years and four months. Ain't God good. Thank you for true love. Until our rocks meet again, shine on. Come visit anytime! You already know where I am. I'm in our big bed.

Will, please leave the door open for me. I will sing the lyrics of Bruno Mars song to you once more when I ascend to the heavens to join you.

Meredith S. Coleman & William E. McGee July 5, 1998

Will holding Glenbruce Campbell's Civil War rifle in his back yard – April 24, 2021 - Meredith and Campbell family picnic. Photo by Tristan Carico, Memphis, TN

Glenbruce is the great, great, great grandson of JAP Campbell. Glenbruce inherited JAP's Civil War rifle and his MS Supreme Court retirement watch.

Will & Meredith, New Orleans, French Quarters, 2002

Traa and Meredith Christmas of 2010

Unc. Henry, Traa kneeling, Boobie front, Dickey, Meredith, Will, Poncho rear, July 20, 2013 Meredith 50th BD Barbeque
Photos William and Meredith McGee Family Collection

Meredith's birthday celebration, 07.20.2021, organized by Jessica, left front, Neko, Jaylon, Man Man – front right Vickie, Joseph, Meredith, Calla, Loretta (Rick's widow) – rear

"Tribute to Rick"

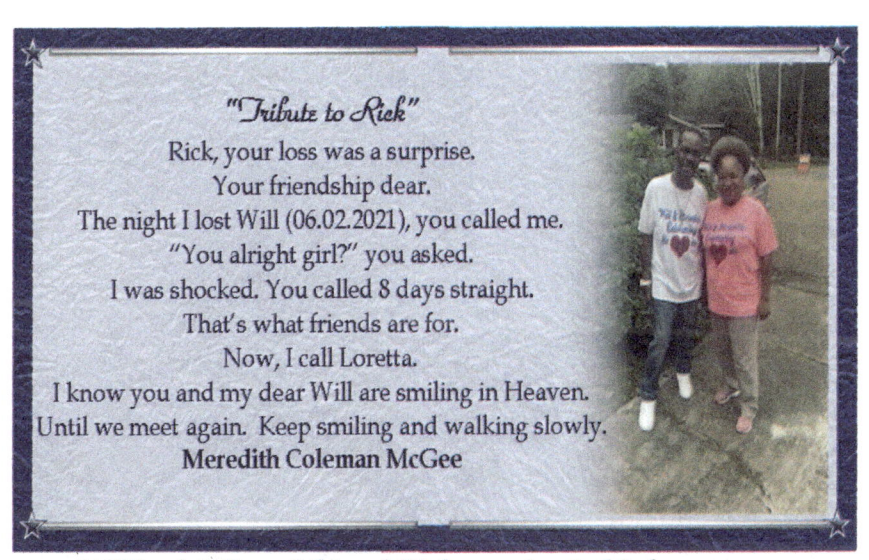

Rick, your loss was a surprise.
Your friendship dear.
The night I lost Will (06.02.2021), you called me.
"You alright girl?" you asked.
I was shocked. You called 8 days straight.
That's what friends are for.
Now, I call Loretta.
I know you and my dear Will are smiling in Heaven.
Until we meet again. Keep smiling and walking slowly.
Meredith Coleman McGee

Will's childhood friend Rick was buried July 10, 2021.
Tribute in Rick's Funeral Program.

Lisa, Meredith, Vickie, & Poncho at Rick's Funeral 07.10.2021

Special Collections Library at Ole Miss. Oxford, MS. *James Meredith: Warrior and the America that created him* and *Odyssey* by Meredith Coleman McGee are housed in Special Collections. Student Poet A'Mya Jones took the selfie.

Eva, DD, and Will at Everett Meredith's repast in Georgia.
Heron Bay Cottage Club Center, Locust Grove, GA 04.09.2018

Meredith, Hazel (mama), Gordie, and Eva at Will's repast.
Gordie had jokes. June 10, 2021

Meredith took Will to dinner on Father's Day 2016

Will & Meredith's 20 Wedding Anniversary, 09. 25. 2019
Judy & Mary - Claudel & J-Boy, & Charlet Meredith
Photos William and Meredith McGee Family Collection
Vow Renewal Celebration

Will & Meredith's back yard - 20th vow renewal Sept 25, 2019

Helen and DL Govan's 70th Wedding Anniversary. June 2019
DL Govan married Will and Meredith, 09.25.1999
Will and Meredith rear

Meredith, Big Bad Bobby Rush (Blues Mega Star) and Will

Mary Hardy, Meredith center, Lynette Stafford

Joe, center, Will, right at Little Sister's repast 03.30.2012

Dwight Johnson's Funeral Will, left front, 05.18.2019
Charles Marshal, front center, black suit died 09.21.2021

Stylist, Grandma Beulah, Meredith, center, Will, Buffalo, NY

Left, Man Man, Meredith's Birthday 07. 20, 2021 Jaylon front Meredith, Christie, Shirley, LaRonda, and Vickie – Chuckles

Parham Bridges Park at the pavilion, Thur. May 6, 2021,
<u>Stand Up, Speak Up Rally 4 Peace</u>
United call against gun violence in the Capital City
Better Men Society members discussing crime intervention
Open mic - 3 minutes per person

Will's younger sister Karen McGee Smith remembered Will's sayings in a post on Facebook: 1. "Finna' go make this dollar holler." 2. "That dog ain't gonna' hunt." and 3. "I'm finna' go to the Ponderosa." I'm adding several sayings: 1. "I ain't gonna' fatten no frog for no snake." 2. "Long story short, I can't tell it all." 3. "You can't pick your family." Will nicknamed Karen "Karen Earl McGee." There are at least four men with the middle name "Earl" in William Earl (Big Will/Willie) McGee's downline.

>William Earl McGee Jr.
>William Earl McGee III
>Kenneth Earl McGee
>Kenneth Earl McGee II

Big Will's name was misspelled on his birth certificate. It was spelled Willie Earl McGee. Will's surname was spelled "Magee" instead of McGee. Will recalled, "Grandmama said, "They wouldn't correct the errors and that's how much they cared about us.'"

I loved every inch of Will's earthly existence as he loved me. I miss Will. Our spirits remain joined.

I hope every reader enjoyed *Every Inch Love Will*.

All the way up. Will's cellphone ringtone

[Every Inch Love Will - Meredith Etc](#)
Make comments on the book page.

Stand Up, Speak Up: Rally 4 Peace, Grove Park Pavilion 05.22.2021
Will, right, holding Pastor Patricia William's dog, Ella, far right.
United call against black-on-black violence in the Capital City
Will played baseball and other sports at Grove Park in the 1970s.
Sports was a haven for Black boys.

Every Inch Love Will

Meredith's birthday 07.20.2018 – Will with concert goers

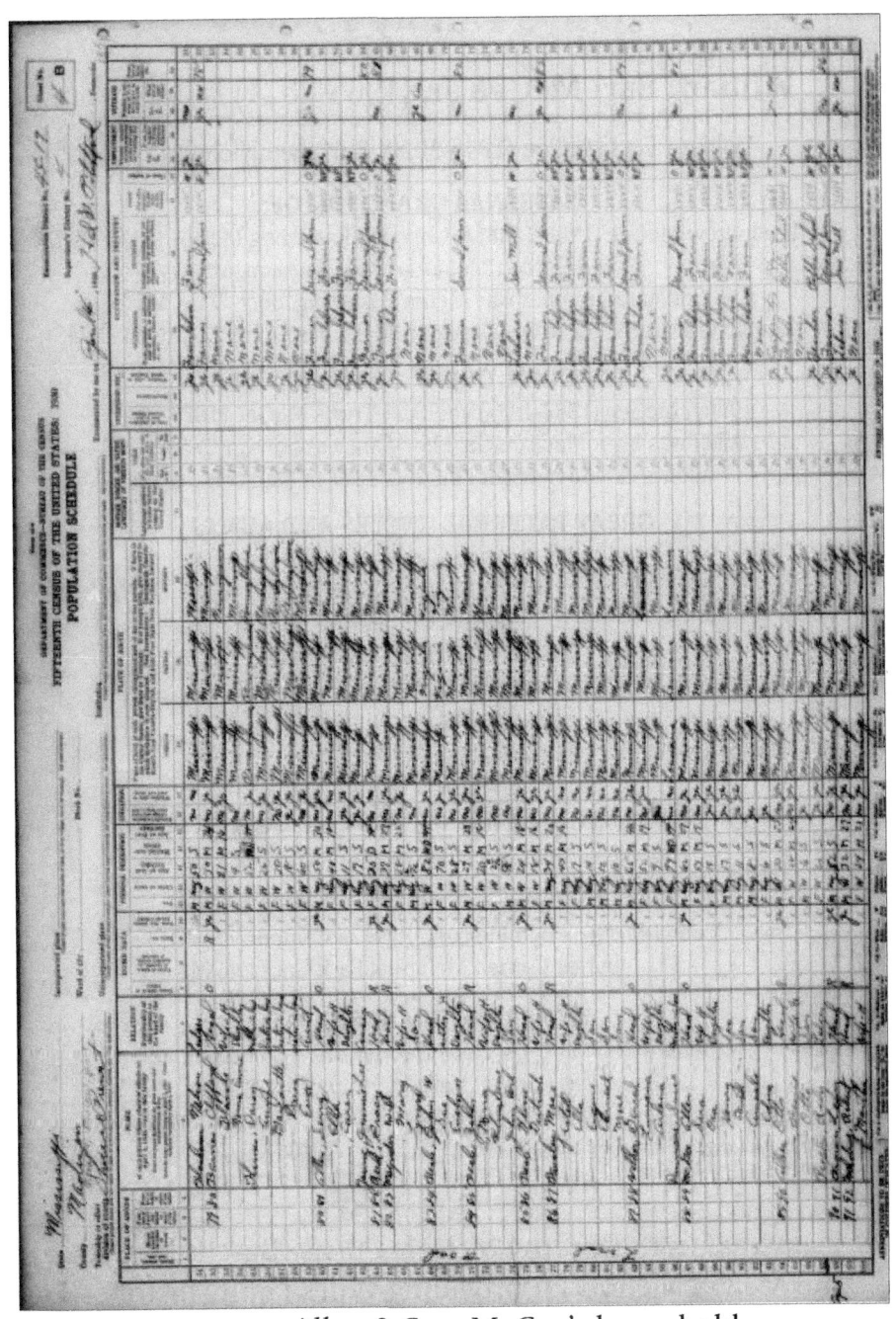

1930 census Allen & Sara McGee's household

Will's Family History

William Earl McGee Jr. (1965-2021) is the son of:

William Earl McGee (1946-2020) & Melvin Nichols (1946-)

PATERNAL GRANDSON OF:
Leeandrew McGee (1908-1988) & Christine Easterling McGee (1912-1995)
buried Garden Memorial Park, Jackson, MS
Christine's mother was Mattie Easterling, born D'Lo, MS
Christine's sisters: Beatrice, Gertrude, Mary Easterling, Mendenhall, MS

PATERNAL GREAT-GRANDSON OF:
Allen McGee (1868-193_) and Sara Travis McGee (1877-194_)
Allen was born Madison Co, MS—Sara was born in Canton, MS
Allen and Sara married March 3, 1897 in Madison Co, MS

GREAT PATERNAL UNCLES AND AUNTS
James McGee, (1898-_)
Eddie McGee, (1899-_)
George McGee, (1901-_)
Clodeal McGee, F (1902-1942)
Chester (Crack) McGee, (1906-1979)
Eleanor McGee, F (1910-_)
Ora McGee, F (1911-1998)
Henry McGee, (1912-1978)

David McGee, Canton, MS 1918-1986, Cook Co, IL
Slaughter and Sons Funeral Home, Chicago, IL

Ameal McGee 1922 Sharon, MS 1988 Cook Co, IL

Edna McGee Pugh Fleming, F (1924 Canton, MS 2018)
buried Garden Memorial Park, Jackson, MS

MATERNAL GRANDSON OF:
Johnny Nichols (_) & Elena George, 1927-_ Jackson, MS
Elena was born in Jackson, Hinds, Mississippi
to Augusta (Gus/Big Daddy) George and Magnolia (Big Mama) George

Many thanks to Dorothy McGee, Curtis (Butch) McGee, and Melvin Nichols for providing Will's family history facts. Some dates are estimates taken from census records.

Edna McGee's 1944 Madison County, Mississippi marriage record lists her mother Sara McGee as alive and her father Allen McGee as deceased.

ABOUT THE AUTHOR

Meredith Coleman McGee is an author, poet, book publisher, lecturer, and small business owner. Her works include *Baby Bubba and Kay, Juneteenth: Freedom Day, Midnight Moon, Odyssey, Nashida: Visits Mississippi's Old Capitol Museum, James Meredith: Warrior and the America that created him, Nashida: Visits the Smith Robertson Museum, Nashida: Visits the Mississippi State Capitol, Married to Sin, Casada al Pecado, My Picture Dictionary, and My First Book Series*. McGee is the widow of William E. McGee Jr. She resides in Jackson, Mississippi.

[Meredith Coleman McGee, Author/Acquisition Editor/Publisher | Meredith Etc](#) Visit the webpage!

ENDNOTE

[i] John G. Neihardt. Black Elk Speaks. Being the Life Story a Holy Man of the Oglala Sioux. Pages 1, 5